CW00504182

IN THE CATACOMBS

Chris McCabe was born in Liverpool in 1977. His three poetry collections are *The Hutton Inquiry, Zeppelins* and *THE RESTRUCTURE*. He has recorded a CD with The Poetry Archive and was shortlisted for the 2014 Ted Hughes Award. McCabe's prose has appeared in numerous places including *Poetry Review, Manhattan Review* and *Unbound*. His work has been described by *The Guardian* as 'an impressively inventive survey of English in the early 21st century.' He works as the Poetry Librarian at the Saison Poetry Library.

ALSO BY CHRIS MCCABE

POETRY

The Hutton Inquiry (Salt Publishing, 2005)
Zeppelins (Salt Publishing, 2008)
THE RESTRUCTURE (Salt Publishing, 2012)
Whitehall Jackals with Jeremy Reed (Nine Arches Press, 2013)
Pharmapoetica: a dispensary of poetry with Maria Vlotides (Pedestrian Publishing, 2013)

PLAYS

Shad Thames, Broken Wharf (Penned in the Margins, 2010)

In the Catacombs

A Summer Among the Dead Poets of
West Norwood Cemetery

Chris McCabe

Penned in the Margins
LONDON

PUBLISHED BY PENNED IN THE MARGINS
Toynbee Studios, 28 Commercial Street, London E1 6AB
www.pennedinthemargins.co.uk

All rights reserved
© Chris McCabe 2014

The right of Chris McCabe to be identified as the author of this work has been asserted
by her in accordance with Section 77 of the Copyright, Designs and Patent Act 1988.

This book is in copyright. Subject to statutory exception and to provisions of relevant
collective licensing agreements, no reproduction of any part may take place without
the written permission of Penned in the Margins.

First published 2014
Second edition published 2016

Printed in the United Kingdom by Lightning Source

ISBN
978-1-908058-19-5

This book is sold subject to the condition that it shall not, by way of trade or otherwise,
be lent, re-sold, hired out, or otherwise circulated without the publisher's prior
consent in any form of binding or cover other than that in which it is published and
without a similar condition including this condition being imposed on the subsequent
purchaser.

Friends of
West Norwood
CEMETERY

The author and publisher gratefully acknowledge the financial assistance of the
Friends of West Norwood Cemetery in the production of *In the Catacombs*.

Contents

ACKNOWLEDGEMENTS

Thanks to Jane Millar for inviting me to take part in *Curious* in 2013. This book couldn't have been written without Colin Fenn's help in linking me up to the poets, enriching my journey with anecdotes of the dead and Victorian history, and for taking me deeper into West Norwood Cemetery than I ever thought I'd go.

In the Catacombs

A Summer Among the Dead Poets of

West Norwood Cemetery

Dedicated to my dad, for bringing poetry home.
Your books on my shelf.

DOCUMENT A : INITIAL STATEMENT

My body, my work. My body of work. Its complete dissemblance is a universe of anti-matter. I write & it adds molecules to my presence : water & acids in all of my written pages. What's left of my blood, my cells, my tissue. I'm a quantity man. I start each day holding an iPad to the sun.

The phone rings after midnight. It's sat there for months in its plastic torso, limbless & cold, curled up in the recovery position.

Hello, is that The Poet?

The voice sounds like it hasn't spoken for some time, as if it's forgotten how to inflect, to make its emotion known. Lack of ictus. The line crackles like an old analogue recording.

Who is this? How did you get my number? How do you know I'm a poet?

This is your poet. I just wanted to say that I'm glad you're coming to find me.

Part 1

How to be Magnificent

Are you too deeply occupied to say if my Verse is alive?
Emily Dickinson, letter to T.W. Higginson, April 1860

The Living Dead

When I spoke of fame I was not thinking of the harm it does to men as artists: it may do them harm, as you say, but so, I think, may the want of it.

G.M. Hopkins, letter to R.W. Dixon, June 13th 1878

I WENT INTO THE CEMETERY because I wanted to find a great lost poet. I wanted to find an original voice: unknown and overlooked for centuries. I wanted to give my ear to their music, to listen for its hiss and cadence in the still-smouldering remains of their white ashes.

I have always enjoyed setting myself a question within set parameters and the parameters here are clearly defined: London's Magnificent Seven cemeteries. In order of creation they are: Kensal Green (1832), West Norwood (opened as the South Metropolitan Cemetery in 1837), Highgate (1839), Abney Park (1840), Nunhead (1840), Brompton (1840) and Tower Hamlets (1841). *In the Catacombs* is the first stage in the journey to search the remains — skeletal and textual — of the poets buried in these isolated parts of London. That search begins here with the 40 acres of West Norwood Cemetery, positioned in a straight southerly line between London Bridge and Crystal Palace: themselves both structures born of the same Victorian industry.

Is the survival and celebration of dead poets' work always to do with their innate, natural talent? And are the rewards always doled out fairly, with the most gifted receiving fame and fortune? The playing field shifts across the sediment of years, the goal-lines slide into cobblestones. It is a recognised fact that women poets were not published because they were women, working class poets were deprived of opportunity and time, but will this be proved with the dead poets I find across these seven London cemeteries?

There are two kinds of maps I'm interested in; two distinct but related architectures. The first is that of the cemeteries themselves, built between 1832 and 1841. In 1832 Parliament passed a bill encouraging private cemeteries to be built on the outskirts of London. This was in response to the explosion of the London populace and the increasing epidemics contaminating the water supply. The population of London doubled between 1801 and 1841, and wherever life thrives so does the death count. In 1852 the small churchyards were closed to new deposits. Dickens wrote a paper called 'City of London Churches' (published in *The Uncommercial Traveller* in 1860) in which he talked of these churchyards as relics, out-dated burial grounds for past generations:

> No one can be sure of the coming time; but it is not too much to say of it that it has no sign in its outsetting tides, of the reflux to these churches of their congregation and uses. They remain like the tombs of the old citizens who lie beneath them and around them, Monuments of another age.

Having been pallbearer for Douglas Jerrold at his funeral at West Norwood, Dickens knew painfully well that the new age of burial had arrived in London. In fact, he had been an advocate of the General Cemetery Company, a group of businessman who had come together to address the problem of burial space in London through entrepreneurial action. This problem became critical, especially after the outbreak of cholera in 1832, yet the business venture also offered an opportunity to those who saw profit in death. One facet of Dickens' genius was that he lived through this age of mass change and development whilst also being able to handle and understand what this change meant: a rare kind of mind which I'll be looking for in the dead poets of West Norwood Cemetery.

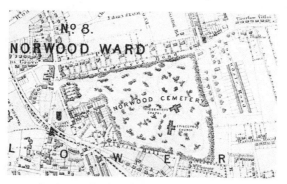

Stanford's map of West Norwood Cemetery, 1876.

Sanitation for the living was not distinct from the dispatching of the dead. London's new cemeteries created a whole new way for the living to experience death. West Norwood itself was inspired by the Gothic splendour of the Père Lachaise in Paris; the lavish architecture of the headstones and mausoleums — as well as the Doric columns and underground apartments of the catacombs — invited a leisurely voyeurism within these suburban spaces. All of the Magnificent Seven became playgrounds for the middle and upper classes, particularly at weekends when they were one of the few places where it was socially acceptable for women to visit alone.

The privilege of being buried in West Norwood did not come for free. The first of the seven cemeteries was built near Kensal Green in 1832. What followed was a virtual monopoly on burial in London run by joint-stock companies who maintained and devised the new rates of costs until the Metropolitan Internment Act of 1850 put the onus back into Government hands. There was no straightforward erasure of social classification under this new management of death; the democratic properties of the earthworm was something for nature to enforce later. At West Norwood the rich could secure extravagant family catacombs: vast underground libraries in which bodies were placed inside lead-lined editions for future browsers. In contrast, graves could be bought cheaply in the common ground of the cemetery.

Not all of the seven cemeteries were laid out in such a way as to confirm the social status quo; Abney Park in Stoke Newington was created as a burial ground for dissenters, taking over the role of Bunhill Fields (closed to burials in 1854) where that great defier of parameters, William Blake, was at last laid squarely in the ground. Blake, and the dissenters that followed, made a declaration against the rules of Christian burial: you never got my mind and you won't get my body. Although the work of a poet can be created long before the world is ready for it, the body itself can never be anachronistic: the earth receives it shortly after its function has ceased.

The unknown poets I hope to uncover will always be shadowed by the celebrated dead poets who have made the 'canon' of English Literature. I call these The Living Dead, poets not only with flora-strewn monuments in London graveyards but also blue plaques across the city. There are dozens of these celebrated writers, though my chosen ones — the ones by which I'll measure the work of the poets I find in West Norwood — are drawn from the inspiration and excitement their work has given me over the years. This is Poets'

London, the London in which the names of the still-read poets have been hewn into the physical city: Blake at Peckham, Apollinaire in Stockwell, Rimbaud in Camden. Their names are plated into stone. It is impossible to walk the course of the Magnificent Seven — 'like a jet-black necklace around the throat of Victorian London' (Lucinda Lambton) — without keeping an openness to the synchronicities between the physical location of these cemeteries and the legendary lifetime activity of the poets beyond their walls.

The underground river Effra provides a strong metaphorical connection for my journey. One branch of the river once rose in Upper Norwood and flowed beneath the ground that became West Norwood cemetery, before being diverted in the 1830s. Joseph Bazalgette constructed his London sewerage system in the mid-19th century and incorporated flows from the Effra into new drainage pipes (made by Doulton). Myths, like culverts in the landscape, gather underground force: they become fact. There is one story of a coffin floating down the Thames which was then traced back to an undisturbed grave at West Norwood. The ground beneath the coffin, it was argued, had collapsed and the coffin had fallen into the subterranean Effra and floated away. In death nothing remains still: atoms disperse, flesh disappears, the ecosystem thrives on decay. All of the dead poets of the Magnificent Seven might be static in their armadillo-poses, huddled for eternal silence, but their coffins have the capacity to move at force into the free-flow of the Thames. This is called readership.

Sweete Themmes! runne softly, till I end my Song. Edmund Spencer's conceit uniting the Thames and the idea of his poetic immortality into one stream is a powerful one for my story. His poem, he suggests, will flow for as long as the river flows; his words will be as lasting as the landscape of London. Is it possible to re-enact the myth of the dead body floating underground down the Effra to the Thames, replacing the real body with the poet's body of work?

We read Victorian poetry through the backward-facing lens of Modernism — what is it that keeps certain poet's work alive in our consciousness while others die off, like unwatered creepers around the frame of the 'canon'? Like the miles of houses built upon the ever-sliding foundations of London clay, the canon of poetry is never secure: found voices resurface, their physical construction often brought to light through recovered texts. There is also the significance of time: poets whose writing was out-of-synch with their period wait quietly for the faculties of their readership to catch up. They have gone forwards, as Henry Vaughan puts it, into a world of light. We follow after them with dim torches.

I picture the bodies of the poets across the acres of London's cemeteries: some cremulated to white bone, others long furrowed into the caverns made by the scavenging fox. I see their skulls like hollowed-out music boxes, once patterned with the stress-patterns of their poetry — the urgency of their poetics — now set into the sediment-layers of brown. What separates them from their neighbouring cadavers is that they tried to play the intricate musical keys of poetry; to attempt to connect their minds-at-play with the work of other poets and offer it to readers as something pleasurable or meaningful that could be taken into their lives. They wanted to be known for the clarity and power of their thoughts captured in the wired mesh of metrical language. My search will take me forward into the cemetery towards the specifics of their burial locations and back into collections and online to find their extant work.

I am also aware that I should be hesitant about the likelihood of finding great work — I've come across enough poor poetry in my time. At worst, the dead speak in a language that was not their own; their words are subsumed by the idea of what poetry at their time of writing was *supposed* to be. Many failed poets make the mistake of seeing the history — and the present condition — of poetry as in stasis, though the poets I admire most have pushed against their present and by doing so have opened up new technical possibilities for later generations. I am not looking for a great Victorian poet: I am looking for a great poet who lived through the Victorian period.

So much of 19th century poetry never woke up to the rapid pace of the century and the necessity to address this in new artistic forms. To find a language to complement the urgency of social change. Bernard Richards in *English Poetry of the Victorian Period* 1830-1890 talks of how there were 'a variety of strategies adopted by the poets faced with the challenging and alarming modern world, ranging from acceptance and acquiescence on the one hand to hostility, protest and evasion on the other'. I'm thinking about this when Ted Hughes — now vaulted in stone at Westminster Abbey — speaks out from the radio, a voice trapped in analogue now flowing digitally, and describes the work of Hungarian poet János Pilinszky: "he has produced no such thing as an 'occasional poem'… He writes, as he says, only what he cannot not write, like a chess player he moves only when he must and as he is forced. 'I would like to write', he has said, 'as if I had remained silent''. It is this kind of urgent silence I hear in the work of the West Norwood dead: I am their audience and the pre-event tension has a kind of electric hush.

Gerard Manley Hopkins captured his struggle with God in his invented technique of Sprung Rhythm; Lord Tennyson contained his wrestling with new scientific knowledge in the compact meta-poetic lyrics of *In Memoriam*; Robert Browning compressed his allegory of Darwinism into the colloquial syntax of 'Caliban Upon Setebos'; Emily Dickinson condensed awareness of her own mortality into oblique lyric poetry. These are not poets who had a Fairy Land idea of the place of poetry in the crashingly modern world they lived in; instead, they created new forms in which to capture the modernity of their crises.

These poets faced the phantoms of convention head-on and their poetry still reaches us with their crises alive and mutating inside its glass case. They never tried to make the complexity of the world heel to the false ringmaster of bombastic language. These are poets who were aware that art doesn't have a need to draw *conclusions*. They understood that a poem is a live place to push around a dilemma: the liveness of the thought and the capturing of emotion is more significant than any outcomes that can be foil-wrapped for the reader . Style is of primary significance. There is the double-fold delight of viewing something *living* through the glass of a plinth, unexpected amidst the dried-out husks of Victoriana, but the viewer notices that the plinth-glass is not clear: the artist has treated it with their own unique handling of language. We look at their concerns through these flourishes and unexpected technical decisions. The dilemma and the language became the same thing; condensed into the poetry that only that poet could make in that way. The dancer and the dance are one, to paraphrase Yeats.

We live in good times for discovering dead poets. The internet has turned poetry into widely-available data, making the possibilities of hearing these dead poets' work possible again. Whole books, forgotten by the culture and shelved in one or two libraries across the country, have been digitised and made available online.

The skulls of these poets — once filled with their decisions and preoccupations — are seen to spring new roots from the soil packed into them or else to be a playground for idle crustaceans. The page of their work traps the synapses of their mind and their metrical gifts; we can hold up the skull for inspection or toss it back into the earth. What drives me towards all of these hours spent in the cemetery, approaching the mid-point of my life, scratching around headstones and committing to the likely reading of whole swathes of doggerel? To risk all this time following maps of burial plots into overgrown corners and reading epics that thump out in monotonous iambic singsong? The straightforward answer is this: I want to discover a poet who deserves a whole new readership. I feel most alive when reading incredible poetry.

Before I start to walk it is important to set out the criteria by which I'll know when I've found a poet worth shouting about. The poets I've mentioned above establish the kind of relationship with society and stylistic originality that I'm looking for; a poet who's an innovator, who creates new forms or adapts pre-existing ones in such a way as to allow their urgent need for expression to manifest in a style that is honed for their distinct purpose. Urgency is important. Although this is something everyone feels and often drives people to create appalling poetry, when it's captured in unique metrical rhythm it becomes the monosodium glutamate for which we will return again and again. If the poet is a Victorian — and as burials take place at West Norwood each week for those who have rights to the plot my poet might even be contemporary — then I'm looking for a Victorian whose work could bridge between their period and the later advancements of Modernism. A poet who scores their page with a future DNA. The work needs to contain *something which I can't get anywhere else.*

The poet should be a cipher of their zeitgeist: the complexities of their once-present world should play through them. It takes an incredible mind to allow an often factitious, changing and unresolved social fabric to manifest whilst resisting the temptation to pick a side or make a judgement. Shakespeare is the prime example. He existed in a hinge between a feudal and early modern world with the old strictures of place and social position eroding to present new possibilities and unforeseen crises of existence. He allowed his characters to dress outside their birth-rank, to redress and cross-dress. Bastards prospered and princes fell. Yet Shakespeare so often refused to make a point about any of this. He showed the possibilities within the prism of language in which all various viewpoints could be accepted at the same time. He didn't use language to complete our thinking for us.

This is not to say I'm not interested in the personal crisis of my lost poet. In a sense all personal crises are bound with the politics of the time. Hopkins's dilemma can be read as the closeting of a gay man who would never have found personal fulfilment in a repressive Victorian society. Tennyson's *In Memoriam* is a very personal attempt to deal with the new knowledge brought forth from Charles Lyle (and others) that the comfort of the afterlife is based upon a fallacy for which religion no longer offers solace. Ted Hughes' account of Emily Dickinson's concerns captures her relationship with the society that engulfed her: 'The Civil War was melting down the whole nation in an ideological gamble of total suicide or renewal in unity. The Indian tribes and the great sea of buffalo waited on the virgin plains, while Darwin wrote his chapters. The powers that struggled for reconciliation in Emily Dickinson were no less than those which were unmaking and remaking America'. Rimbaud undid himself from society in order to see the limits of civilisation. He had to create the prose poem to do this.

The great poet is bound to their time but compelled to invent the poetry of the future. The fractious paradigms of society creates few individuals who write literature that contains the old and new worlds at the same time; that captures the real complexity of existence as it is lived in its historical moment. As T.S. Eliot has put it: 'Not only every great poet, but every genuine [poet], fulfils once for all some possibility of the language, and so leaves one possibility less for his successors'. My journey begins with the assumption that there is a real possibility of finding a forgotten poet's work that, on reading, will become something I can't imagine having lived without. I remind myself, while preparing my rucksack for my first visit to the cemetery, that Hopkins wasn't published until 29 years after his death and that Emily Dickinson's first book came out four years after she'd expired. In both cases the survival of the work was determined by those who happened to have copies of the poems and a personal belief they should be published. But what about those who died without these posthumous editors?

It is this possibility that takes me to the cemetery.

Getting Curious

Wind oozing thin through the thorn from norward.
'The Voice', Thomas Hardy

CURIOUS IS AN ANNUAL SITE-SPECIFIC ART TRAIL that invites artists to respond to West Norwood's cast of burials and its Gothic landscape. This summer I have been commissioned to create a work for *Curious*, the only poet amongst 20 artists. Last year I visited Sophie Herxheimer's papier-mache of Mrs Beeton which she had placed in residence at the graveside of Mrs Beeton herself. There were busts everywhere: Sophie told me how a Frenchman with mental health difficulties had hidden himself in the bushes but then emerged to try and cover up Mrs Beeton's papier-mache breasts with her own papier-machine arms. A Victorian gesture against the contemporary artist. There were poems that day too with Sophie's words hanging from the trees, like leaves in the trellis-patterns of the branches. Pages fluttering in the breeze. That too was an invitation into poetry.

When I was much younger I went to visit Père Lachaise with my wife Sarah and was frogmarched from the grounds for drinking alcohol at the grave of Jim Morrison. (I had already visited Apollinaire and had enough inspiration to write the poem about his grave that went into my book *Zeppelins* — it only occurs to me now that this growing obsession with dead poets is just that: growing). The influence of that earlier Parisian cemetery, built in 1804 in the outskirts of the city, is a big influence on Sir Willian Tite's design of West Norwood Cemetery. Built in a similar Gothic style, the main paths of West Norwood Cemetery form an arterial structure around the grounds — the map looks like a heart under the duress of a cardiac — and smaller tributaries form short-cuts between the pathways or simply end, as if abandoned. The cemetery exists in an organic tension between overgrowth and control. Whole tombstones are often covered in bramble and wildflower allowing the voyeur to feel what it must be like to be dead here, to have succumbed to a natural landscape that never sits still.

Many of the monuments stay where they fall. After decades of harsh weather the weak points of structures are found out and gravity steers them earthwards. There is restoration and conservation too, a landscape and history that is loved by the Friends of West Norwood Cemetery and nourished as a living place for people not only to learn about history but to be saturated to the bone with the weight of it. Walking into West Norwood is to enter an enclosed world of Victorian invention and design. The class system is played out in the hierarchy of expensive mausolea and invisible common burials. It isn't just the rich that speak to us: if you listen closely enough, the poor whisper through the subterranean network of

Exhumation of Rossini at Père Lachaise in 1887. Photograph: Pierre Petit.

worm-thin tributaries.

   And I am here to listen. My work for *Curious* will be to allow the poets to speak for themselves, through the words they left behind them, on the earth.

DOCUMENT B : DE-ACCESSION

Creation : all my new acts, all their old words. Completion before beginnings : the idea its own music. Its newness, its oldness.

The voice called me Poet : do the dead know who is read in the future? Am I on the list?

Things have being going well : journals, commissions, collaborations. The plagiarism is well in the past. Eliot said great poets borrow. The publication of that poem was an administrative oversight.

It was not an administrative oversight.

The poem was a conceptual gesture about where we are with poetry. It was my own brand of Recontextualised Magnificence. I was doing with text what Warhol had done with Campbell's soup : pouring the words onto the transparent plate of the page. Capturing the colour of what was already there, as my own, forever.

I take two important steps : check online for fake IDs and buy a heavy duty garden spade.

West Norwood : even the whispering sound of the soft consonants allures. It keeps the fizzing neon and the spores of fried chicken out of my senses. I check the notable burials : a dozen dead poets. John Yarrow, William à Beckett, Greek poet Demetrious Capetanakis. One of them could be me.

John Yarrow is a good name to assume. Not too far from 'marrow' — he wears his bones well — but it also sounds honest, believable. Earthy : of-the-earth. The incident with the British Library hasn't proved a set-back until now. Research, to the genuine poet, is like the chemical chart of paint properties to the artist : informative but stifling. Experience is my moodboard, adrenalin underpins my stress patterns.

I keep the razor blade tucked inside the flysheet of my first pamphlet, *Bold Transparencies*. I call up only one book — I should have asked for the eight — & take it to desk 215 in Humanities B. It opens on a bold serif font, red and black, redolent of Baudelaire's *Fleur de Mal*. Rimbaud would have known that. UNE SAISON EN ENFER. I want the title page, not the poem : a more potent framing.

I open *Bold Transparencies*, finger out the razor, delicate as a dried-out moth & pass it across direct — pages touching — from my first published work to Rimbaud's. The thick unfoxed slightly-yellow page sears silently as the razor cut downwards. Synchronicities : his page had been cut to the slightly larger A5 format of my own. It tucks inside, an offsprung addendum, a foundling reclaimed. A single word in rough rural French drifts across the chilled library : sorcieres.

It took them a year to find me. Me, him, who I was then : Dr Alex Lumis. All my related cadences. Litmus. Lumens. Luminary. Luminescent. They took all my borrowing rights away but my success came later : they went on to acquire my collection, *Selections*.

I've re-registered under my pen name, Daniel Rush. How could they keep me out when they've collected my books? And now research will be the steering process to creation, I'll walk past Paolozzi's Newton in the forecourt under the name of who I really am. The Writer.

Research : I don't believe you, I believe you.

The problem with poetry is that nobody knows who's really good because nobody knows what poetry is anymore. Formalist, conceptualist, vispo, post-avant, linguistically innovative. So much work firing its disparate strands down non-fibre optic cables. False poets, first passing off puerile emotions under the anachronistic ruse of Jacobean drama; cashing-in on Hopkins in half-formed sequences. But where are they in all this, what does 'the poet' think about anything, what's their take on the world? We come to great poetry — & this has always been the feedback on my work — because what we want from it are the same four important questions asked in original ways. These false poets asks the old questions in the old ways & in a borrowed music that they're never going to pay back. The kind of hybridity that adds dashes of fine wine into carafes of budget merlot.

John Yarrow : my enemy, my shadow.

I would rather spend my days making extant texts completely my own than working in these cross-pollinated half-formed atrocities. It's impossible to learn anything from my contemporaries. My line is underground. The body of work I learn from is in the earth. Where I've come from and where I'm going to. Out of contemporary days shrouded with blackness rise clumps of mud sinewed with elm roots. Greatness illumines over centuries — not in a reading in the upstairs room of a pub.

My body, my poems. My process, my resolution. I pass into a new age, untouched but lit by the shock of new contexts.

Welcome to your immersion, my genius.

Part 2

The Millionaire's Cemetery

Old Yew, which graspest at the stones
That name the under-lying dead,
Thy fibres net the dreamless head,
Thy roots are wrapt about the bones.

Alfred Lord Tennyson, *In Memoriam*

Bones Built in Me: Measuring the Dead Against Hopkins and Dickinson

Bones built in me, flesh filled, blood brimmed the curse.
  Selfyeast of spirit a dull dough sours. I see
The lost are like this, and their scourge to be
As I am mine, their sweating selves; but worse.
    'I wake and feel the fell of dark, not day', G.M. Hopkins

AS FAR AS THE LOST GO, Hopkins got lucky. Or rather, *we did*. Following his death in 1889 it took 29 years for his first book to be published and this was only possible because of the perseverance of his friend, and fellow poet, Robert Bridges. Bridges kept hold of the texts — slowly anthologising a poem here, another there — until the world was ready for them. At the time of them being published Bridges himself was 74. Hopkins' life as a dead poet depended on his friend's ongoing commitment to his work and his good health into old age. Even genius requires its fortuitous contingencies — there is no automatic right-of-place in the afterlife of readership.[1] Hopkins wrote before his readers were ready, but time and perseverance have connected him to his readership. Robert Bridges' dedication to Hopkins provides inspiration to my cause.

Hopkins is the Victorian poet by which I'll be measuring the work of the poets of West Norwood. He is a luminary, the most original poet amidst the fog-shadows of so much bombastic Victoriana. Hopkins discounts any notion that sensationalism alone can carry a poet's reputation into the future canon. His life was quiet, a Jesuit who had little in the way of relationships and who died in his early forties. As far as biographies go his approach to living was as unlike his near contemporary Charles Algernon Swinburne as it is possible to find.[2] Yet Hopkins' existence was fraught with the oscillating mood-swings of the manic depressive. His endorphins were dappled with both ends of the mood spectrum.

I have a further attachment to Hopkins: he spent a short period of his life in Liverpool as a Jesuit at the church of St Francis Xavier, only a mile away from my current home. He wrote his poem 'Felix Randall' there. His place on the physical map of London is Stratford, in the east, where he was born, a short distance from Tower Hamlets cemetery (known locally at the time as Bow Cemetery) which was opened in 1841, three years before Hopkins' birth.

Hopkins captures the urgency of the seemingly quiet life. His poems contain the crises of his thought and nerves through varying degrees of linguistic rapture and despair. After outraging his parents with a shift from Anglicanism to Roman Catholicism he decided to dedicate his life to the Jesuit brotherhood and it was during this time that he made the decision to burn the poems he'd written up to that point. Hopkins felt that the focused, reflective and disciplined life required of him as a Jesuit would be impossible to level with the public and ego-driven life of the poet. He referred to their burning, in a letter, as 'the slaughter of the innocents'. As with all quiet lives — and as Lyndall Gordon has argued for the intensity of Emily Dickinson's — it is often the little-known aspects of a poet's life that supply the emotional force behind the work.[3] Words born of silent struggle cannot be held in the hand and filtered through the fingers.

Hopkins felt his life keenly — nothing unusual there — but

his gift was to express it in compacted lyric poetry that flowed with a unique gift for rhythm and phrasing. Hopkins called this uniqueness *inscape*: the distinct essence which make every organic thing *that particular thing*, and not something else. The manifestation of that thing in the world — the way it moves or makes itself known — was defined by Hopkins as *instress*. As I walk through West Norwood, moving among the great flat slabs of tombstones, and the columnar shadows set from slowly decaying mausoleums and memorials, his singular way of looking at the world gives me a way of describing how I will know the great dead by their work. The urgency and originality will have its own unique *inscape*; the language will be the instress for that statement of singularity:

> Each mortal thing does one thing and the same:
> Deals out that being indoors each one dwells;
> Selves — goes itself; *myself* it speaks and spells,
> Crying *Whát I dó is me: for that I came.*
>
> I say móre: the just man justices;
> Keeps grace: thát keeps all his goings graces;
> Acts in God's eye what in God's eye he is —

Here, in his poem 'As kingfishers catch fire, dragonflies dráw fláme', Hopkins delights in veering from the expected iambic flow of the line: the accents above both 'what' and 'do' invite emphatic stress above the alternating syllables that the Victorian reader would have been poised for. By the second stanza the reader is forced into a molossus: a rush of rising syllables: 'Kéeps gráce: thát'. Hopkins places a colon before the third stress to force the reader into placing emphasis on 'that' (this technically breaks the musical foot — the unit of three stresses — yet the poise of waiting for the third stress, which the reader can see on the page, forces the line forwards in its rush of three rising syllables). The sibilants of 'selves', 'speaks' and 'spells' further propel the urgency with which nature once more confirmed for Hopkins that he was right — it is the absolute uniqueness of each individual species or form that gives the world its variousness. As such, Hopkins makes clear that each poet's work should strive for this kind of uniqueness of expression too.

Gerard Manley Hopkins. (Photograph: unknown.)

In this poem two of the vaguest words on the poet's palette — 'what' and 'do' — are double-stressed with both an accent above them *and* italics to bring to the fore the strength of the poet's conviction. Hopkins makes the point through performing it: the rulebook for poetry is open to re-evaluation. And Hopkins, despite his dappled faith, was a poet of conviction: his feelings of uncertainty have the same weight of feeling as those of his unequivocal joy or despair. When it later came to questioning God in his 'terrible sonnets' he did so with such inquisitorial vigour it was like he had found a way of sending waves of light-particles back to God's eye.[4] Hopkins' authority of voice is powerful enough to speak in direct terms with the unjust creator. Whenever we read this poem — and Hopkins made it known that his poems should always be read aloud — it is Hopkins' distinct voice and expression that breaks through the silence. We hear the inscape of his nature, and how that nature after years of thought and wrestling within the strictures of Victorian poetry — a goldfinch in the catacomb — trills along the trellised branches of his unique poetic instress.[5]

Hopkins's uniqueness resides in his invention of sprung rhythm. This was the phrase he used to explain his use of irregular stress patterns in his work. Although not wholly unique (he had found examples in Anglo-Saxon poetry and the Elizabethans) it was an approach to rhythm that was wholly out of favour with the Victorians. The classic line of a Victorian poem was measured out in regularly stressed syllables, like heaps of coal dispensed door-to-door. Although there were always exceptions to the metrical hegemony (Coleridge's conversational poems, moments in Leigh Hunt's work and Christina Rossetti's sinuous and innovative 'Goblin Market') the standard poetic line would follow a set musical pattern usually amounting to eight, ten or twelve syllables. The majority of Victorians, by the point of Hopkins' development into the lyrical flex of his strongest poems (1876 onwards) were trying to drumbeat with a basic set of tally-sticks.

I know it's perhaps unrealistic to find another Hopkins — he is a poet that might come along once a century. Yet the survival of Hopkins' corpus is itself so tenuous — if Robert Bridges had died younger then the work would have died too — that there must be, if not in these cemeteries then in other parts of England, poetry of great value that has been lost to its rightful readership. It just may be that West Norwood Cemetery is the resting place of this overlooked author. I look at the map of West Norwood with the arrows placed above each poet's burial plot: reading Hopkins readies me for the deep reading each of the poets deserves. Hopkins turned language into a material that could almost be handled and provides a useful way of measuring what might otherwise be little more than clods of soil and air.

For variants to this approach we would need to look across the Atlantic. Walt Whitman was breaking new ground with the extended free verse line, self-publishing an edition of just under 800 copies of his new epic *Leaves of Grass* in 1855. Emily Dickinson was compacting whole spectrums of emotion into minimal lyrics presciently suggesting the compressed approach of Imagism. Like Hopkins she saw very little of her work published in her lifetime.[6] Her poems are emotional and urgent: she wrote 362 in 1862 alone. As she wrote to T.W. Higginson, a future editor, and — it's been suggested — inspirer of romantic passion: 'My little force explodes'.[7] As with Hopkins, Dickinson was alert to each moment as having the potential to transform the everyday into the poetic. She explained this in another letter, sent to her friend Abiah Root when the poet was just sixteen: 'Let's us strive together to part with time more reluctantly, to watch the pinions of the fleeting moment until they are dim in the distance & the new coming moment claims our attention'. Dickinson was fixated with the brevity of life and knew she had a little time — a short lifespan — to mark her existence through poetry. There is a tension in her work between the awareness that she has no control over the body's ailments but does have control of a powerfully unique voice able to condense the speed of life into lasting literature.

Dickinson's writing processes reveal how closely this relationship between poetry and life were for her. The publication of *The Gorgeous Nothings*, the facsimiles of her envelope poems, beautifully documents the overlap of the poet's material existence with her philosophical and poetic concerns. Many of her poems were first written on the backs of envelopes from letters that she'd been sent. They would then be copied into letters and later redrafted into little booklets (which have become known as 'fascicles'). When we read the finished versions alone we miss this incredible opportunity to witness the creation of the works at their precise point of inspiration. Dickinson would always keep a pencil in her right-hand pocket and write on whatever scraps of paper were available to her. Seen like this, her poems exist on a different spatial plane. Many of her poems invite a conceptual engagement with an ontological issue such as Darkness. The reader's mind is free to oscillate and wonder in this open space between meanings. What's incredible about Dickinson's work is how the brevity of the lyrics can allow for so many ramifications of meaning: they are cups containing oceans.

Envelopes have words (and hoped-for worlds) inside. They are flat yet openable. Dickinson's poems are held together through axiomatic reductions and strong visual imagery; they are both physical and mental worlds. For Dickinson, sometimes language is inherently unable to contain the speed of the world around her; at other times it offers a handle on that world that has proved immensely useful for later readers and for subsequent poets. Objectivists such as George Oppen and Lorine Niedecker; poets associated with Black Mountain College, such as Robert Creeley and Denise Levertov and contemporary Americans like Fanny Howe and Peter Gizzi, have all learned from her. Words and worlds collide and intersect.

'Tried always / and Condem / ned by thee', draft on both sides of a cast-off envelope, Emily Dickinson, 1882. (Amhurst College: Emily Dickinson Collection.)

Death and life cohabit opposite sides of the same envelope. She suffered illness all her life and lived in awe and suspended horror of when her time on earth would end. Her desire to be filled with whatever joy and fresh surprise life could offer is captured in the envelopes as a powerful series of stills. This late poem of 1882, 'inscribed on both sides of a remnant of a cast-off envelope', is written within the folds of the separate sections of the envelope. Typically of Dickinson's ability to condense difficult thought into seemingly simply lyrics, the poem is written not just in the three visible sections of the surface of the envelope — moving as if in a whorl — but also on the back of the envelope. The poem becomes four-dimensional:

Tried always and Condemned by thee
Permit me this reprieve
That dying I may earn the look
For which I cease to live —

In the draft version the word 'Permit' is both underlined and capitalised. From the perspective of the poet, the text can be read in different ways: a statement to God in that she says she might at last see him in death; a desirous call to a potential lover (at this stage she was in a relationship, mostly through correspondence, with Judge Otis Lord, to whom she sent some letters suggesting that she was contemplating marrying him); and, significantly from my perspective, as a poet whose readership was yet to arrive. Perhaps I am already so far lost in my own grand project that I read in Dickinson's work a knowing sense of her future fame? That as I prepare to spend a summer digging around dead poets of potentially far less ability, I need to hear a voice of complete confidence so that I'll know what the true and rightful poetic ego sounds like when I find it? I hear in Dickinson's poem here a direct address to the unknown reader she never had in her lifetime. Through choosing not to publish Dickinson knew that she would have to "cease to live" in order to speak to this reader. She creates a plea to us to complete the circuit required to do justice to her work which we have fulfilled as being part of her mass readership: the gap in time closes and her distinct voice continues to be heard.[8]

Dickinson, an American who never visited England, will be close to me in the cemeteries of Victorian London: she is also a reminder of the disappearance and posthumous celebration of incredible poetic work written during the period of the Magnificent Seven. Her own tombstone is often shown online with stones balanced along the top-edge. At Dickinson's funeral Emily Bronte's poem 'No Coward Soul is Mine' — a favourite of hers — was read. This poem also captures Dickinson's fierce certitude in the longevity of her own work (Bronte herself died at the age of 30):

> There is not room for Death
> Nor atom that his might could render void
> Since thou art Being and Breath
> And what thou art may never be destroyed.

Although the first editions of Dickinson's work sold well, and initiated the cult that developed around the poet, it would take over half a century for the poems to be published as the author intended. They were restored to their refractive elliptical edge in the Thomas H. Johnson edition of 1955. For a poet so sensitive to the specifics of cadence and meaning, this was a long time to wait for her poems to be seen as she intended, with all their clotted and compact language distilled to shot-glass strength. The work instantly felt modern as it forced the slant edge of her rhymes — and the shards of her broken punctuation — into the exposed senses of the reader.

Britain was in a slower lane in the mid-19th century. Tennyson had picked up the mantle of the laureateship after the death of Wordsworth but had also reached the apex of his output with the publication of *In Memoriam*. This sequence had taken him 17 years to write and manages to enmesh Tennyson's disparate feelings of loss around the death of his friend Arthur Hallam and the previous Biblical certainty that the world had not been created along God's Timeline. The work is incredible for its playing out — almost in real time — of the social crisis of religion through the mind of one man. Here, in section three of the poem, Tennyson manages to condense this complex struggle — specifically around the knowledge that the sun was one day destined to burn out — into dense and memorable lyric poetry.

> O Sorrow, cruel fellowship,
>> O Priestess in the vaults of Death,
>> O sweet and bitter in a breath,
> What whispers from thy lying lip?
>
> 'The stars,' she whispers, `blindly run;
>> A web is wov'n across the sky;
>> From out waste places comes a cry,
> And murmurs from the dying sun:
>
> 'And all the phantom, Nature, stands—
>> With all the music in her tone,
>> A hollow echo of my own,—
> A hollow form with empty hands.'
>
> And shall I take a thing so blind,
>> Embrace her as my natural good;
>> Or crush her, like a vice of blood,
> Upon the threshold of the mind?

This extended image of sorrow which begins with 'the Priestess in the vaults of death' — an apt image for the beginnings of my journey into Anglican grounds — speeds across the spheres, unpinning the stars from the fabric of religion, to end inside the poet's mind, at the centre of the exact synapse that is attempting to process the devastating reality that he'll never see his friend again. It is this tension between giving in to sorrow, and rage against the fact that the sorrow is born through the lack of rational solace, that drives the powerful final image of this poem: grief pounds through the temples of the poet, 'a vice of blood', that stills his brain as if shot from the inside.

The brilliance of *In Memoriam* doesn't reside in technical innovation; the form for the poem (largely iambic tetrameter in an alternating rhyme scheme of ABBA) had been around since the 17th century. Yet Tennyson shows his awareness of this through a meta-poetic commentary on the nature of grief in relation to the writing of 'verse'. The tangible force of this grief finds potency through the tension between such a simple rhythm and its inevitable failure to contain in form the poet's fierce questioning. Tennyson arrived before us in asking what straightforward poetry can actually *do* to offer any balm to personal tragedy in an unsettled world. This lends the poem a tremendous force it might otherwise lack:

> I sometimes hold it half a sin
>   To put in words the grief I feel;
>   For words, like Nature, half reveal
> And half conceal the Soul within.
>
> But, for the unquiet heart and brain,
>   A use in measured language lies;
>   The sad mechanic exercise,
> Like dull narcotics, numbing pain.
>
> In words, like weeds, I'll wrap me o'er,
>   Like coarsest clothes against the cold;
>   But that large grief which these enfold
> Is given in outline and no more.

T.S. Eliot wrote that *In Memoriam*' is not religious because of the quality of its faith but because of the quality of its doubt. Its faith is a poor thing, but its doubt is a very intense experience'. This doubt extends to the faith that the poet might have in the writing of traditional verse.[9] Despite this, Tennyson's live struggle with faith and grief and his ability to condense these complex issues into searingly compact lyrics provides a measure for how the traditional form — when used with intelligent self-awareness — can be incredibly powerful and lasting. *In Memoriam* was massively influential on later poets who often recycled the form without declaring to the reader that it was 'only' verse.

In Memoriam was published in 1850 and represents the apex of what Tennyson would achieve. In later years Tennyson's work began to sound like just that: Tennyson's work, pastiches of himself. He never struggled so energetically with ideas and personal grief as he did with those earlier poems. In his novel *Ulysses* James Joyce has his younger self Stephen Dedalus refer to him as 'Lawn Tennyson': the dead Laureate's poems politely begin to ping the ball of each regular stress across the net of each end-rhyme. Hopkins, in 1864, wrote a letter to A.W.M. Baillie, saying: 'Do you know, a horrible thing has happened to me. I have begun to *doubt* Tennyson'. Hopkins then goes on to separate the language of verse into different categories, lumping Tennyson in with what he calls Parnassian: 'It can only be spoken by poets, but is not in the highest sense poetry... [it] is that language which genius speaks as fitted to its exaltation, and place among other genius, but does not sing'. Hopkins quotes a section of Tennyson's 'Enoch Arden' to demonstrate what he means by Parnassian writing. Tennyson, whilst inventing new games in 'The Princess' — and extending way beyond singsong in his poems of grief for Arthur Hallam — had become a spent force.

Byron had earlier envisaged that there would be a backlash to the advances made by the Romantics. Although there is diversity across Victorian poetry, before Hopkins there was little in experimentation that could threaten to break the shackles of staid and complacent verse. The wild flourishes of Swinburne who worked in powerfully looping long lines and made an assault on many prevailing moralities, would engage a whole younger generation for whom Tennyson's medievalism had come to seem quaint. Swinburne's first books were published in the mid-1860s. In a society torn with massive change through industry, technology and moral order Swinburne was a poet who seemed mad, bad and dangerous enough to make this new world order heel to his poetic direction. He had an incredible energy which led to him writing far too much and to varying standards: one has to stand in the strange secluded garden of his work (images prevail of hidden landscapes in Swinburne's work) and hope to be made delirious through the bite of a mosquito or midge.

Robert Browning, arguably the greatest ever ventriloquist of the human voice and mind, worked within regular metrical forms but allowed his characters to give away their uniqueness so effortlessly. It took decades for a readership to catch-up with his experiments in this form. Although we now take the dramatic monologue as a standard sub-genre within the poet's range, it took Browning's Victorian readership 35 years to begin to listen with sensitivity to the nuances of his work.[10] There were few rewards for innovation. This was the glass ceiling — without the scale and well-structured dome of the Crystal Palace — that the experimenting Victorian poets often found their voices rising up towards, and then returning, accompanied with cacophonous groans of disgruntlement.

Yet it is Hopkins who will be the poet against which I will measure my new discoveries. Hopkins was the first Modernist and the most radical poet of his age. His poetics — the clutter of firmly held beliefs about writing that he kept tucked inside his collar — and the way he realised these through his work, were at least 50 years ahead of his contemporaries. Hopkins was also a Victorian. As such he suffered for the precocity of his gift, and for his foresight for what poetry might become (based upon a line through the past that he saw himself working in — a live node in a long network of dead minds). As many of his contemporaries — including those he was friends with, such as Dixon and Bridges — were measuring out syllables like cough candies, Hopkins' art was led by his instinct and an inversely atavistic desire to *listen* to what poetry from the future might sound like.

Before moving into the cemetery it is worth hearing Hopkins in full: for the trellis-work of his lineation (within the line as well as at the end) and the music created from the compounding of separate words into one new construction; for the careful orchestration of pace through stresses and monosyllabic words and the doubling of the lines in which each segment (separated by the straight dash) has up to five stresses (the same as a standard line of iambic pentameter) to create an incredibly modern sense of nature in flux, of atoms in perpetual movement. Hopkins' genius is to create a language that flexes with the landscape he is invoking, and it is this understanding of the particle nature of existence — and of language — that gives the poem its physical qualities. The suppleness of the language allows the moment of Hopkins' immersion in nature — and in poetry — to unfold line by line:

Cloud-puffball, torn tufts, tossed pillows | flaunt forth,
        then chevy on an air-
built thoroughfare: heaven-roysterers, in gay-gangs |
        they throng; they glitter in marches.
Down roughcast, down dazzling whitewash, | wherever
        an elm arches,
Shivelights and shadowtackle ín long | lashes lace,
        lance, and pair.
Delightfully the bright wind boisterous | ropes,
        wrestles, beats earth bare
Of yestertempest's creases; | in pool and rut peel
        parches
Squandering ooze to squeezed | dough, crust, dust;
        stanches, starches
Squadroned masks and manmarks | treadmire toil there
Footfretted in it. Million-fuelèd, | nature's bonfire burns
        on.
But quench her bonniest, dearest | to her, her clearest-
        selvèd spark
Man, how fast his firedint, | his mark on mind, is gone!
Both are in an unfathomable, all is in an enormous dark
Drowned. O pity and indig | nation! Manshape, that
        shone
Sheer off, disseveral, a star, | death blots black out; nor
        mark
            Is any of him at all so stark
But vastness blurs and time | beats level. Enough! the
        Resurrection,
A heart's-clarion! Away grief's gasping, | joyless days,
        dejection.
            Across my foundering deck shone
A beacon, an eternal beam. | Flesh fade, and mortal
        trash

> Fall to the residuary worm; | world's wildfire, leave but
>   ash:
>   In a flash, at a trumpet crash,
> I am all at once what Christ is, | since he was what I am,
>   and
> This Jack, joke, poor potsherd, | patch, matchwood,
>   immortal diamond,
>   Is immortal diamond.

As with Dickinson, Hopkins suggests that his work will be his afterlife: the poem is the 'immortal diamond' of his own resurrection. A brief comparison with the extracts quoted from *In Memoriam* above shows how radical this poem is. Even its typographical flourishes across the page suggest that the poem has come from another epoch: that of the American Modernism of e.e. cummings or the hybrid prose of James Joyce. Where Tennyson mourns the loss of a world in which God's reign over its original creation has been lost, Hopkins takes the disparate micro-elements of nature as evidence that there must be a true God. Hopkins' representation forecasts the phenomenological writing of Merleau-Ponty who would, 60 years later, attempt to define our beings in a world of rapidly changing perspectives in which each object is a 'mirror of all others'. Hopkins' experiments in perspective and parallax are suggestive of a philosophical and existential approach to poetry in which it is possible for the reader to move around inside the poem, buffeted from image to image, taking a new position with each new line.

    As my journey takes me backwards into poetry but also forwards into the cavernous, dilapidated and beautiful cemeteries of London, I imagine the map of past poetry like a transparency above the physical map of the city. Hopkins uses a similar image in a letter to poet Robert Bridges in 1878, comparing the initial distaste the reader might experience for his work to Thames water: a strange taste that could sweeten into a delicacy:

> Now they say that vessels sailing from the port of London will take…Thames water for the voyage: it was foul and stunk at first as the ship worked but by degrees casting its filth was in a few days very pure and sweet and wholesomer and better than any water in the world. However that may be, it is true to my purpose.

Robert Bridges, a future poet laureate, was reading through the shifting clay, trying to understand his friend's work and not view its radical nature as careless: yet it took even him many years to acclimatise to the shifts and turns of its rhythms. In his life Hopkins trudged through ever-lowering expectations that he would see his work well-received. His fame and place in poetry have arrived belatedly, not only through genius and originality, but through chance and the perseverance of a friend.

The successful poets of their time die more slowly after their body's cease. The self-righteous — those who built an ego through the lavishness poured upon their work — disperse into atoms afterwards. Coventry Patmore — a poet who was successful in his time but rarely read at all these days (mostly due to the dated Victoriana of his rhythms, rhyme schemes and overall earnestness of address) — wrote to Hopkins to express his view that he should slow his work down to the plodding horse-power of traditional verse than the pylon-lit kinetics that was confusing his contemporaries. Patmore described Hopkins's poetry as 'veins of pure gold embedded in masses of impracticable quartz'. Ironically — and Patmore is beyond many of his contemporaries in at least being cognisant of Hopkins's 'gold' — Hopkins has later proved to be not impracticable but incredibly useful to the modern poetic mind. His poetics have freed up generations of poets not to repeat the trod, trod, trod (to paraphrase a Hopkins' poem) of staid versification and to attempt to write distinctively and musically, creating rhythmic clusters of sound which expresses the creator's unique, probing mind. Hopkins' sprung rhythm has invited poets to use their own inner ear. Further generations have dropped the end-rhymes and regular syllables within the line and have run with the musical beat to suit their purpose. Poets like Patmore would have been happy to live by candle-light.

There is also in Hopkins the honest scream of a mind in crisis. He wrote his four terrible sonnets on two sides of a sheet of paper, saying to Bridges that 'they were written in blood'. They were never published in his life. As we are still struggling to find a platform for advancements in mental health, Hopkins' poems have proved helpful to those who have also been to the terrible places inside themselves. These poems feel contemporary and unlike anything else in the Victorian canon. The direct appeals to God and the reader extend into the materiality of the language and pound with the temporal pain of real despair:

> Not, I'll not, carrion comfort, Despair, not feast on thee;
> Not untwist — slack they may be — these last strands of
>   man
> In me ór, most weary, cry *I can no more*. I can;
> Can something, hope, wish day come, not choose not to
>   be.
> But ah, but O thou terrible, why wouldst thou rude on

me

Thy wring-world right foot rock? lay a lionlimb against
    me? scan

With darksome devouring eyes my bruisèd bones? and
    fan,

O in turns of tempest, me heaped there; me frantic to
    avoid thee and flee?

Why? That my chaff might fly; my grain lie, sheer and
    clear.

Nay in all that toil, that coil, since (seems) I kissed the
    rod,

Hand rather, my heart lo! lapped strength, stole joy,
    would laugh, chéer.

Cheer whom though? the hero whose heaven-handling
    flung me, fóot tród

Me? or me that fought him? O which one? is it each one?
    That night, that year

Of now done darkness I wretch lay wrestling with (my
    God!) my God.

Hopkins in his buttoned turtleneck jacket and swept-over fringe looks more like a fifth Beatle than a Jesuit poet, yet his fame arrived with no mania on earth (outside of his mind), no storming of America. What spurs me is the awareness that Hopkins had only one true reader in his life in Robert Bridges, and if Bridges hadn't understood his work, or had died younger — or not been so compelled to act — then Hopkins too could have become another skull buried in the ground: the awesome and terrifying music of his mind silenced forever.

White Addition Black Total: The Poets of West Norwood

I ARRIVE ONE MORNING IN APRIL, two months before the trail opens, holding a list of 12 names. Colin Fenn, of the Friends of West Norwood Cemetery, has sent me a list of Notable Burials (there are over 300 entries of Norwood burials in the National Dictionary of Biography) and from that I've been able to draw up a list of the names that have POET — the warning sign — next to their short biographical entry. The dates of the poets spread across the Victorian, Edwardian and Georgian periods, and Modernism — to the contemporary. The mystery of obsession instantly gives way to specifics, so that the cadence of each name suggests possibilities for the rhythm of their work, even before I've read it. I've made the decision to find their place of burial before engaging with their writing: the cemetery at this stage is a level playing field. Any of the twelve could be the poet I'm looking for.

> SIR THOMAS NOON TALFOURD (1795-1854)
> SAMUEL LAMAN BLANCHARD (1804-1845)
> WILLIAM À BECKETT (1806-1869)
> THOMAS MILLER (1807-1874)
> JOHN OVERS (1808-1844)
> JOHN YARROW (1817-1898)
> MENELLA BUTE SMEDLEY (1819-1877)
> THEODORE WATTS-DUNTON (1832-1914)
> EDWARD JAMES MILLIKEN (1839-1887)

H. D. Lowry (1869-1906)
Demetrious Capetanakis (1912-1944)
Sydney Carter (1915-2004)

The landscape murmurs with the satisfaction of small creatures: wrens, grasshoppers, rats. The whole earth seems astonished by the heat after weeks of rainfall. The staff at the reception — used to fielding enquiries from the recently bereaved — offer placatory smiles at my introduction that I'm a poet working on the *Curious* trail. The phones are ringing with relatives seeking to witness their own names pressed into the stone of forebears. Dates for new cremations need to be made: this is the urgency of real life and death business.

Still, they give me access. I've got the plot numbers of the 12 poets; each number has a preceding two-digit area code, followed by the precise five-digit number of their location. The man behind the desk — large build and shaven head, his PC screen running a McAfee firewall two centuries on from the after-hours' body snatchers — explains in a slow and high-pitched Cockney that I'll have to trawl through drawers of A1 plot maps to find the location of each body. There's a further obstacle too: there are precise numbers for each poet but no system for finding the numbers within the cemetery itself. Burial plots don't run in sequential order. The only way of locating a specifically numbered grave is to look behind each headstone until you find one which has its code pressed into the stone and then hope that the one you're after is somewhere close.

The other obstacle is that although the poets have all been allocated a plot — the physical space that was perhaps overlooked in the generational anthologies they never appeared in — they won't necessarily have a headstone. Their skeletons alone will X the spot.

With the gravitas and slow-tread of one who knows how to pace out their working day, the reception desk man shows me the cabinet of maps. He takes out the first map — John Yarrow — and then sets up a table in the back office for me to locate the next 11. This unearthly football team, taking the deathly route through life — poetry, the art of the suicidal (if mid-20th century America is the measure) — and the promise of the life-after-death path. The receptionist's coat is hanging from the coat stand over the desk I'm working at: it has a West Ham badge on the collar.

It takes two hours to locate the map locations of each poet (Sydney Carter was cremated and has none; I draw a blank for Blanchard). The photocopier whirrs painfully to copy the corners of the maps as the phones ring for relative reconnection, for cremation before combustion...

At last I'm out again, under the sun, heading past the rows of real dead. Like all-night libraries crashed by overuse I find the seeming impression of order — and the reality of randomness —

Plan of John Yarrow's grave in West Norwood Cemetery.

exciting. Frustration follows hot on enthusiasm: the realisation that plot numbers on the maps are not linked to any literal borders between one section and the next. There is no sign that says WELCOME TO YOUR POET.

I do, however, have hope of finding one of my poets today. I follow the left-leaning path that winds from the Gothic terrain to the Greek section, looking for Demetrious Capetanakis. He is one of only two of the poets of the 12 of whom I've heard (the other being Theodore Watts-Dunton); I've seen his books in my place of work, living on the shelves of the Poetry Library, on the fifth floor of the Royal Festival Hall.

The Necropolis rises, a Grecian landscape in south London. The mortuary Chapel of St Stephen's looks down over the rows of regulated single graves outside of the enclosure, its Doric structure encased in white and honey limestone. The boundary of the Necropolis is marked by draped urns, foliated crosses and hollow iron railings. I step inside.

What is immediately odd is how the imagery of Greek mythology has been replaced with scenes from the Old and New Testament: Adam and Eve in the Garden of Eden, Noah building the Ark, the baptism of Christ. Etched into St Stephen's is a piece of text from I Corinthians: 'for the trumpet shall sound and the dead shall rise'.

The Greek Necropolis was founded shortly after the gates of the cemetary opened; the owners were approached by the Brotherhood of the Greek Community in London who were looking for a Greek Orthodox burial ground. A lease was signed on Christmas Eve 1842 and expensive, brick-lined graves were sold in perpetuity for £5 5s. In its first century there were over 350 filled plots and 1,000 funerals. Today new internments only take place in the plots for which people have burial rights.

Capetanakis' stone is a simple, rectangular slab with Greek and English text. It has lost its upright place on the earth and has collapsed flat, mimicking the position of the coffin beneath. The burials on either side highlight the simplicity of his. On the right is the mausoleum of Xenophon E. Balli (died 1877), an impressive four-column temple with marble walls and a plinth at the top of the steps. The chamber has slate shelves for 12 coffins, though the original entrance has been walled in. Balli owned a shipping fleet and was later a director of the Metropolitan Provincial Bank. He is buried with his sons, one of whom was a patron of Whistler.

On the other side of Capetanakis lies Nicolas Ambrosios Mavrogordato (1851-1890). His grave is marked with a high Calvary cross within a cast iron screen on a low stone wall. His plot is described in West Norwood's guide to the Greek Necropolis with extreme love: 'It incorporates curling tendrils, fronds, bulbous openwork finials and a florid iron cartouche with raised lettering'. Mavrogordato has a Liverpool connection: his family had settled there before making their way to London.

Capetanakis stares directly up at the sky, as the degrading properties of the sun beat down on it. He was born in Smyrna in 1912, the son of a doctor who died when Capetanakis was just 10. Soon afterwards the Turkish army occupied Smyrna and he fled with his family, studying in Athens and later in Heidelberg under Karl Jaspers. The philospher's views on making the leap of faith he called Transcendence would be influential on Capetanakis, as would his view on 'Existenz': the freedom of authentic experience. These became Capetanakis's ideals but personal and societal obstacles would collude against him: the outbreak of the war, depression and blood cancer.

Capetanakis moved to England in 1939 after winning a scholarship from the British Council to study at Cambridge University. In his short, restless life he moved between conflict and conflict, the effect of which was a kind of internalisation of the tension induced

Plan of Demetrious Capetanakis' grave in West Norwood Cemetery.

from warring nations. He arrived in London as the war broke out, working briefly for the Greek Embassy's Press Office. It is incredible that the poems — and also the essays — he wrote from this period until his death in 1944 were written in a language that was new to him. He became a protégé of Edith Sitwell and became associated with the Bloomsbury Set.

Bold claims have been made for his poetry: 'a lasting contribution to the rich heritage of English poetry' (Philip Sherrard); 'Demetrious Capetanakis was a being of rarest integrity in thought and feeling, and he was incapable of writing anything for the sake of 'making literature" (John Lehmann); 'Of the loss of those poems that will never be written I cannot trust myself to speak' (Edith Sitwell). I look at his photograph on the cover of his book *The Isles of Greece;* he has what the Victorians would have called a handsome forehead. His eyes, whether opened or closed, have an impressive dreaminess, as if he thought only in symbolist expressions. He looks like a snooker referee from the by-gone days of the gentleman's game.

Demetrious Capetanakis. (Photograph: Dr John Capetanakis.)

His hairline has well-tended widow's peaks, wider than the middle-pockets on the billiard table. A second photograph inside *A Greek Poet in England* show his clear, unblemished skin. The suit jacket and tie were a constant adornment. I take a look at the titles of the essays that Capetanakis wrote: he covers European literature from Russia, Greece, Germany, France and England. Dostoevsky, Greek ballads, Stefan George, Proust and Charlotte Brontë are all approached from various perspectives.

If Capetanakis turns out to be the great lost poet of West Norwood then I can't — as the quotes above suggest — lay claims to be his discoverer. He has been published, discussed and (particularly in relation to studies in 20th century Greek poetry) is still read today. The Poetry Library loan copies of his two books have been checked out 12 times between 1988 and 2002. Here lies an extant poet.

Despite the orderliness of his appearance Capetanakis had arrived in England set upon real experience. He wanted to push his intellect as far as it could go (he was said to have read Proust's *Remembrance of Things Past* 14 times). His essay on Rimbaud (a young homosexual poet, as Capetanakis was, who had also arrived in London intent upon deranging his body and mind and had also frequented the Bloomsbury and the British Library Reading Room) reads like a manifesto that might have been written by the long-dead French poet:

> What matters is not the conclusion we draw — in another moment we might draw the opposite conclusion with equal truth. What is important is to get really interested in such things, to dare to think of them, to dare to face the problem of our existence. Nothingness might save or destroy those who face it, but those who are condemned to unreality. They cannot pretend to a real life, which, if it is full of risks, is also full of real promises.

Capetanakis had received a doctorate in philosophy from Heidelberg University before moving to London in 1939. He died four years later of Leukemia, his body blitzed by its own warring cell. He was 32. Capetanakis had an impressively European mind when it came to his thinking and his poetry was often a way of testing out the strength of his thinking. His respect for deep thought was put under the duress of his strong urge for sensory experience.

A branch snaps behind me: blackbird. The cemetery has its own ecosystem of flora and fauna, a balanced cycle of growth and decay. On the far side of the grounds, two men are hoisting a broken headstone up from the earth. The engine of their truck ticks over, humming across the silent acres.

Capetanakis' reputation hinges on the 17 poems he wrote in English from the point at which he arrived in England.[11] I have brought his poems to read in the cemetery. I read them, ready to be surprised by a respected poet who — like Conrad — had come to London to write in his adopted tongue. What I find is a poet who was yet to find a real focal point for his passions. If he has a subject it is, at a push, London. There is a poem about Emily Dickinson, another about angels. Technically, his curious mind and limitless energy for experience is hemmed in with the limiting quatrains and invariable eight- or ten-syllable lines he chose to write in. Rhythmically, the stresses of his lines are as evenly spaced out as the coloured balls in snooker, pinned on their spots like coat buttons. I feel disappointment sink in me, discovering a poet who rhymes 'silly' and 'Piccadilly' without irony. His use of language hybridises the classic tropes of poetry — Biblical and mythical imagery — with the banal. Capetanakis was set upon making the impressive Europeanness of his mind canter to the beat of traditional English poetry. Rimbaud had infused his spirit in wartime, but there was none of Rimbaud's radical reworking of poetic form as the only container that could do justice to radical thinking. Despite writing nearly 70 years later than Rimbaud, a reader could easily believe that the French poet was a contemporary.

There is, though, amongst the 17 poems a particular one that I read once, and then again. It is one of only two poems that risks an indent away from the left margin of the page. The poem is richer than his others and recalls the Rimbaud essay which had excited me:

> Blond smell of sleeping noon and quenched desire;
> Stillness of clotted sun and limbs that float
> In hairy sweetness, auburn like the fire
> Which licked the lips and glided down the throat,
> Leaving a lump of bliss stuck in the root
> Of coming songs…
>   Experienced by two stones
> Grown in the core of love's transparent fruit
> Round which the burning bee, the summer, drones.

This poem, clearly about gay sex, condenses its imagery in a way that is unresolved and yet compacted enough to excite the synapses with the yoking of seemingly irreconcilable sensory images: 'blond smell', 'clotted sun', 'hairy sweetness'. Nouns and adjectives are potently confused, forced together in asyntactic ways. The suggestion of the poem — a sexual encounter with another man, the real stones of a woodland — are crushed into the overload of the poem's single sentence.

'Experienced by Two Stones' shows what Capetanakis might have gone on to achieve in his writing. I remember that he died at just 32, four years younger than I am now. There is a spark in this poem — the spark of stones that might have led to fire if there was more fuel — that hints towards what might have come next if Capetanakis had lived.

But there is something else that excites me, an idea that seems to break from the inside of the stone in Capetanakis' poem.

I have been thinking about my artwork for *Curious*; perhaps there is an interesting way of taking the poets' words back to them? I need to find the right kind of carriage in which to take their poems to their resting places. The merging of words and stones in Capetanakis' poem presents me with the idea of using stones as the conveyor of their words. Sign-posts for the casual cemetery tourist. I picture the phrase 'clotted sun' etched into a stone.

The blackbird takes flight, its wings a contained forest fire. Its lift-off writes the sky like an exploding text-block.

I follow Capetanakis back to the 1940s, a cultured European confined to the ash-wet streets of wartime London. The war presses in on his mind, even as he tries to focus on his primary love of poetry.

Here he is talking of Rimbaud's *Illuminations*:

> The poet's destructive passion is now directed, not only against the human body, but against all the orders of the world, against the whole world. The 'Illuminations' are an attempt to blow up all appearances, all orders, all forms of the world, which make our happiness. They are an attempt to blow up all happiness and make a work of pure unhappiness out of the debris and fragments of the explosion.

Capetanakis took war as an extension of the emotional urgency with which he was living as a poet. Writing about Rimbaud — a poet at war with his society and its morals, and at war with himself — allowed Capetanakis to use the spectra of the French poet's rising and plummeting moods to articulate the confined mania that the Blitz induced in him:

> The war is very frightening, but it is not frightening enough. The fear cannot go deep enough to shake the mind. The grief cannot go deep enough to make the mind bleed...Human beings are condemned to spend their lives in happiness, that is in the order of the world. World, the opposite of chaos, means order, and order makes us comfortable and secure — that is happy...this unavoidable happiness is our curse....It is an evil power which subjects us by flattering the laziness of our bodies and minds, sends our real self to sleep and sees that we lead a life that is not our own.

There are two lessons here for the beginning of my journey into the lives and stories of forgotten poets: firstly, don't judge the poet's mind by the impression that their photograph makes. Secondly, don't presume a radical mind — and a razor-sharp gift for prose — bleeds with the same alacrity into the writer's poetry. Capetanakis was easily imbued by the tone and style of his subject; when writing about Rimbaud he momentarily became Rimbaud.

Between the stones and the sun: it isn't difficult to feel the passion and urgency of the man even if he never found a unique way of expressing this urgency in his poems. Still, his time on earth was one that has been captured for all its energy, thought and individuality; a man of mythic fire trapped in a well-cut suit. William

Plomer, in recollection of Capetanakis, wrote:

> He was excited by crowded underground trains on
> winter's nights in the black-out. He was excited, as a
> novelist might be, by manifestations of feminine jealousy,
> unusual ambitions, renunciations, hopeless love affairs,
> unpredictable impulses. He was excited not only by films,
> but by the fact that they were visible in dark and crowded
> theatres.

How Capetanakis kept his passions to himself as a gay man in
wartime London is impossible to know, yet that delight in the
body and in chance encounters found expression in the best poem
he wrote. With an increase in the confidence of his success, and the
quicker playback of relaxation that post-war London brought, it is
easy to imagine him going on to write a new body of poems imbued
with his own distinct style and lustre.

Capetanakis has already been found, at least by the few, and
his best poem will prevent him from being forever lost too. I can't
lay claim to his discovery but I can say that he isn't the life-changing
poet I came here to unearth. Time deprived him of the chance to find
the unique, clear voice of his poems. In addition to the poems and
essays there is another aspect of his work which is significant: his
translations, particularly from the Greek. 'Anniversary' by Odysseus
Elytis shows Capetanakis working within the lithe and supple
cadences of the more talented poet:

> I brought my life as far as this
> Point that struggles
> Always by the sea
> Youth on the rocks, hand

To hand with the wind
Where is man going
Who is nothing but a man
Measuring his green moments with
Their coolness, the visions of his
Ears with waters, his remorse with wings
O life
Of the boy that becomes a man
Always by the sea when the sun
Teaches him to breathe forward where the shadow
Of a seagull vanishes

I brought my life as far as this
White addition black total
A few trees and a few
Wet pebbles
Light fingers to caress a forehead
What forehead
The expectations wept all night and no one is any more
No one is

I follow the undulating Ship's Path through deciduous and evergreen trees, looking for the only female of the 12: Menella Bute Smedley. I've no way of knowing if I'm even *near* her plot, the numbers on the backs of gravestones bear no relation to the map. It is no coincidence that the only female poet on my list is hard to find: despite a massive increase in female poets in this period, their books still represented a minority of all published collections. According to research by Catherine Reilly, of the 2,605 poetry books published between 1860 and 1879, 639 were by women. In addition to this, many female poets were categorised as 'women poets' and separated from the mainstream of poetry by men. Women featured little in contemporary anthologies that included both sexes, though this was the beginning of the gender-defining anthology and 'women's poetry' became recognised, and isolated, as its own genre.

Hunger stirs: a welcome distraction. In my bag I have a yoghurt with honey. It's the perfect day for good bacteria and natural sugar to lactate, to run in a sun-flood. I find a gravestone that's pressed flat into a small hill like a black post box and sit on the grass verge next to it. The headstone is for a man who died aged 30, leaving behind a wife and daughter. This was 1980. His daughter would now be middle-aged. I spoon-feed myself the sweet yoghurt.

There is a danger to the mind in hanging around cemeteries. Let's say I am half way through my life — a whole smattering of perfect spring days is left to me. But is there enough time left to squander in the grounds where bodies are laid down in perpetuity? It's too late to go back. The allure is uncompromising: I want to meet my poets. If not today, then soon.

I make a short video on my Blackberry of a mausoleum simmering at the centre of epileptic midges and trundling bees. I shoot in miniature my hand scratching around in the arid earth for stones. I survey the ground with wasp-like scrutiny. When I play the video back later the footage surprises with a hidden soundtrack of a far-off lawnmower murmuring lazily across the grounds of the cemetery.

Summer has arrived.

DOCUMENT C : RESEARCH

Night sweating : I overheat when I'm tired. Like Rimbaud
I don't need drugs for the disarrangement of my senses.
I fall asleep with his poems across my chest : the book
rises & collapses with each breath. I dream that I'm at
a dinner party, in New York — it must be the 1950s — all
around me the poets of the time are wearing black & white
check suits. Berryman, Lowell, a very young Ted Hughes.
There's a song playing but the stylus is stuck in the
groove, repeating the same loop:

> *Dig with me*
> *dig for me*
> *come with me*
> *I'm coming*

The jostling males make way & a woman comes forward from
the far end of the long white room. It's Anne Sexton.
Everyone's laughing. There's a dog yapping around her
ankles. She's much more attractive than in the YouTube
videos. She's smoking. She's smiling through one eye.
She's carrying a jar of gherkins. All the men are laughing,
apart from Berryman, who's observing. She hands me the
jar & says:

> - It's in there
> - What, I ask, laughing : what's in there?
> - Your penis

Everyone in the room laughs. A glass smashes further off
but they keep on laughing. *Find it*, she says.
I take the gherkins out one-by-one, only they're

not full-sized gherkins; they've been cut off leaving blunted bullet-sized pieces. I realise that if I can't feel my penis amidst all the gherkins then my penis must be very small & that's what everyone is finding so funny. I'd never noticed before how the proud gooseflesh of the fruit is similar to that of the penis in arousal. But these gherkins are all made of stone. Hughes is hanging his head, laughing, his face concealed under the vulpine cowl of his hair. Lowell lights a cigarette. I realise that my penis isn't in the jar but that if I was as great a poet as the people in this room then I wouldn't have believed this to begin with & I wouldn't be worried. Anne Sexton says:

    - This is the November of the body. Will you be my son?

The book slides from my chest as I wake : foxing dappled with sweat.
    I pour out some iced water, my shaking hands genuflecting in the light, refracting from the neon of the Dixie Chicken across the road. I flick through channels.
    A car is approaching from a far-off bend, through the country. The camera follows as it passes, up the hill towards the cemetery. Black and white is a good idea : it brings my body temperature back down.

    night OF THE LIVING DEAD

night is in lowercase, OF THE LIVING DEAD is in upper. I press the 'info' button on the remote control.

    In this low-budget, horror classic, seven
    people take refuge in a remote Pennsylvania

*farmhouse as they face relentless attacks
by zombies desperate to eat their flesh.
While trying to fend them off and stay
sane, the band gradually loses the battle
to keep the peace with each other and stay
alive.*

I've seen this before : twice, maybe three times. There's
something different this time though, a new connection.
It's after the brother & sister have laid the flowers
at their parents' grave & the brother is attacked by a
zombie redolent of Samuel Beckett that the synapses start
to connect.

I pick up *A Season in Hell* & read :

*ferocious invalids … in whose blood shall I
walk … let me lift up with a withered fist
in the coffin's lid*

The sister has run from the cemetery, leaving her brother
who's been knocked unconscious by a zombie, & has made
it to an old house where more zombies are walking from
the woods, their shoulders raised, backs hunched, still
wearing the civilised suits of their previous lives.
She tries to make a call but the phone doesn't work.
She runs up the stairs & screams : there's a flesh-eaten
corpse, its white eyes like undigested lychees amidst the
reconstructed vomit of its bashed-in skull.

*They will not kill you any more than if you
were a dead body … I saw myself in front of
an infuriated mob … I am a beast, a savage
… Invalids and old men are so respectable
they ask to be boiled … I will bury the*

dead in my belly

The sister tries to run from the house, straight into the glare of the torchlight of a living man who is running from the zombies. He wants her help boarding up the windows of the house. The sister is in a delirium, unable to function. The man leaves the house, stoves in the head of two zombies with a crow bar. The zombies, like B-list poets, are shuffling in a crowd around the house. The man fends them back with a fire-lit sofa.

> *I saw a sea of flames and smoke in the sky …*
> *a premature coffin filled with limpid tears*
> *… What is rotten must be thrown aside … I*
> *see black in this sunlight! My heart … my*
> *limbs … My entrails are burning … twists*
> *my limbs, deforms me and hurls me to the*
> *ground … Come on, demon!*

The man is explaining how he first came across the zombies, in a service station : there were ten or fifteen of "the things" chasing him, holding it on to the truck "like a moving bombfire". He saw a man screaming. There was no one there to help him. The entire place was encircled. "I realised I was alone, with fifty or sixty of those things just standing there, staring at me".
  I take off my shirt : splash water across my chest. The man drove through them. They just stared. "I just wanted to crush them". I drink the last of the water. Pick up the Rimbaud:

> *A man who tries to mutilate himself is*
> *surely damned, isn't he? I think I am in*
> *hell, therefore I am … the delights of*

damnation will be all the greater … A
pillow is over my mouth … I am certain that
I smell scorched … I am dying of weariness.
It is the tomb. I am going to the worms,
horror of horrors!...The fire rises up again
with its damned.

The man looks like the Jesus in Madonna's 'Like a Prayer' video. But he's not a saint & this is 1968. He hits the woman in the face when she won't stay calm. When they find more people living in the basement he wants them all under his direction. The man is different from Rimbaud in this respect : he was fighting off the zombies while Rimbaud WAS AWARE THAT HE WAS BECOMING ONE.

I open the windows for air : the last-orders strollers following their usual paths home. Compelled by alcohol & the memory of habitude. The habitude of memory.

I write down the title of this art experience I'm living inside : A SEASON IN HELL : THE ZOMBIE MOVIE. Rimbaud had a whole crisis inside his stickleback skull. He was aware he was becoming a zombie, but this was his problem : THE WHOLE ORDERED WORLD OF CIVILISATION WAS MADE OF ZOMBIES TOO. There was the established blood lust of money, morality, custom. Then there was his zombification, the bloodlust of his nihilism, his hate. Unlike the man in Romero's film he had nothing to stand up for, no conviction to keep him sane. He oscillates, reneges on his inner beast, his demons — 'O Happiness, O reasons' he pleads — realising that all his previous poetry is no longer fit to be absolutely modern. He recycles his old work inside this new poem. His past, our future.

I wrote out silence and the nights.

Zombies all around him and taking over his consciousness.
To be ordered is to zombie, to take arms against boredom
is to zombie. 'Morality is a weakness of the brain'.
Happiness, he says, is a worm that eats you from inside
: ploughs holes while you're kneeling to pray in fresh
crisp linen.

> *I see myself again, with my skin eaten by*
> *mud and plague, worms in my hair and armpits*
> *and still bigger worms in my heart.*

Outside there are two men shouting from the doorway of
Dixie Chicken, their mouths full of chicken, hurling
abuse with fists full of bones. I draw the curtains &
turn on the radio: 'consistent reports from witnesses to
the effect that people who acted as though they were in
a kind of trance were killing and eating their victims
caused authorities to examine some of the bodies of
victims; medical authorities in Cambridge have concluded
that in all cases the killers are eating the flesh of the
people they murder.'

Arms are pushing through the boards of the window,
the men in the house are pushing them back the man with
the gun shoots the zombie the camera shows the bullet
pushing through the back of his shoulder in a fistula
of blood   the zombie looks up   a face from West
Norwood cemetery   the face of a poet   the face of
Demetrious Capetanakis

Part 3
Meeting the Dead

The glory of the presence of dead poets
imagined in the presence of the glory of the sky
Algernon Charles Swinburne

EDWIN JAMES MILLIKEN
(GRAVE 15,751, SQ. 11)

DEMTRIOUS CAPETANAKIS
(GRAVE 39,710, SQ. 29)

THOMAS MILLER (GRAVE 2,291, SQ. 7)
JOHN OVERS (GRAVE 576, SQ. 8)

SYDNEY CARTER
(CREMATED, SQ. 38)

HENRY DAWSON LOWRY
(GRAVE 31,654, SQ. 43)

SIR THOMAS NOON TALFOURD
(GRAVE 1,452, SQ. 34)

SIR WILLIAM A'BECKETT
(GRAVE 11,988, SQ. 52/53)

MENELLA BUTE SMEDLEY
(GRAVE 16,536, SQ. 92)

THEODORE WATTS-DUNTON
(GRAVE 11,576, SQ. 97)

SAMUEL LAMAN BLANCHARD
(GRAVE 1,345, SQ. 98)

PLAN
of the
South Metropolitan Cemetery,
Lower Norwood.

Published by
WILLIAM PIPER,
Statuary and Mason.

JOHN YARROW
(GRAVE 19,522, SQ. 122)

Map of the 12 poets' burial plots.

Fragile Egos: Returning Poems to 12 Dead Poets

Surely, after you are what is called "dead", you will be
willing that the poor ghosts you have left behind, should
be cheered and pleased by your verses, will you not? —
You ought to be.

Helen Hunt Jackson, letter to Emily Dickinson, 1884

SOME HEADSTONES ARE LIKE TWEETS. Take this one of Nellie Bacon : 1895-1985. All we know is that she lived that time-span, the scope of two World Wars. The phrase "No regrets" is etched into the stone.

Dead poets are more doppelgangers than ghosts: the blood-kin of the rarely read. At least these 12. Born between 1795 and 1915, 10 of them were previously unknown to me — now I'm standing beneath the Doric arch of the cemetery waiting to meet them. I've found some work by each of them, enough to allow me to select a phrase from each of their poems to return to their graveside. I've taken the idea from Capetanakis and made it happen: two words from each of their poems have been engraved into a stone. I've spent hours in libraries looking for their words, rummaging the dead coals for a few cindering white ashes.

Five of the 12 poets are listed in *The Concise Oxford Chronology of English Verse*, which includes over 3,000 authors and 15,000 works. Having familiarised myself with each poet's work I'm surprised by those who made it in to this canon-defining chronology, and by those who've missed the cut. 'Ephemerality exemplifies the taste of the moment,' the editor, Michael Cox, says, adding that making decisions around what is a 'lasting' work can reflect the significance of its social context as well as its aesthetic merits. I have found that there's a richness to be gleaned just from reading of the experiences of those who lived through the 19th century, though my goal doesn't change: I want to find a genuine and truly gifted artist.

Jane Millar, curator of *Curious*, meets me at the gates, stacking unused packs from another artist involved in the trail who is preparing to occupy the Maddick Mausoleum. Rule Number One of artistic curation, as I've learned — don't be distracted from one artist by another: egos can be as frail as those of the long buried. Jane is an artist who has the vision to allow other artists to explore their visions: she has curated some of the strangest interventions with death that it's possible to imagine.

My work for the *Curious* trail is an anthology of my poets. Anthologies are usually compiled around a generation or movement in poetry. This one is determined by poets who happen to be buried in the same place. I have also made a book, a short anthology, under the title *Clotted Sun* — an image taken from Capetanakis' 'Experienced by Two Stones'. I take his stone to him first, in acknowledgement of

his influence for the idea. I lay it down on his flattened headstone.

The book has been printed as an edition of 50, executed at breakneck speed for today's opening by artist, poet and bookmaker David Henningham. Working with David is to enter into a dialogue in which all book-making dreams are possible — the painful part is having to make a decision. We went through a number of options for what we might do: a flutter-book in which the pages replicate the journey through the cemetery, a book as a map, a book as a set of drawers housing the stones themselves. "It's up to you", he said. The idea of a portfolio in which each stone would be reproduced at its exact size and with the two words debossed into the page, as they are in the stones, won out. We pinned down the colours in a pain-free way, following our instinct for what a book called 'clotted sun' should look like: a three-tone cover and endpaper combination of bright orange (sun), light blue (sky) and brown (stone, earth).

There is not enough said about the real geniuses in the art of bookmaking (Stefan Themerson and Ron King are two of my 20th century heroes) and David Henningham, only in his early 30s, excites with the same boundless imagination for creating the book from the inside out. He is able to make anything, manifesting the spirit of a text in a way that satisfies the eye, hand and mind. The cover is inspired; a gold wave symbolises the arch at the gates of the cemetery, like a pre-digital analogue wave.

Jane takes me to the columbarium where a copy of *Clotted Sun* will rest for two months. A poet's dream: each niche is marked by a letter from the alphabet to aid identification. The legacy of Father's Day last week has been left in cards and gifts perched onto the shelves next to the photographs of the deceased fathers. I think of how I'd taken my five-year old son Pavel fishing that day: five roach, 13 bream and a perch. One niche has a token can of Stella and 20 Marlboros in salutation of a father, gone. With love. Remembered. The Stella has been opened and drunk before being placed on the shelf.

The columbarium was one of the first in the country, after cremation was made optional (Shelley, that sea-wrecked maverick, got there long before when his body was set in flames on the shore). The seventh cremation in the UK happened here. During the bombings of the Second World War the columbarium was hit and and A to L was lost: an alphabet disaster that would prove catastrophic for any dead poet.

I place Sydney Carter's stone in a niche that Jane has reserved for me. Carter was the only poet to be cremated and by far the most recent, dying in 2004. When I was researching his burial spot the receptionist at the cemetery office had offered to give me the contact details for the funeral directors who had taken him away. I declined the offer.

There is an interesting connection between Carter and Capetanakis. Not only are they the only two of the 12 here to have been born in the 20th century (Carter was born just three years after Capetanakis but lived for another 60 years) but their lives came very close to overlapping through their involvement with the Greek Friends Ambulance Unit. Carter had travelled to Greece after the war to help with the Ambulance Unit and it was there, in fact, that his interest in writing poetry began to mutate into songwriting. In 1941 Capetanakis went to Birmingham to help a team of the Friends Ambulance Unit prepare for relief work in Greece in readiness for the country being lifted from Nazi occupation. Here is a direct link across time: two intellectual pacifists sharing a conscientious objection to war.

Carter wrote hundreds of songs including, most famously, 'The Lord of the Dance'. He was astounded by its ever-increasing popularity. He had thought that the idea of Jesus dancing would be taken by the church as slightly heretical and didn't predict its uptake in the church and beyond, through its many pagan versions. Carter had no objection to this: he was, in the loosest — and tightest sense of the word — a songwriter of *faith*. To justify the inclusion of him as one of my poets I follow the thread back to the beginnings of lyric poetry, to Sappho's lyre and the source of the spoken word as accompanied with music. His book *Green Print for Song* was also published by a hybrid poetry/song publisher of the time, Galliard. This book is also in the Poetry Library and — so, it goes — he must be a poet. The loan copy of the book has seen a fair amount of borrowing activity over the years.

Carter has offered his songs as templates for others to adapt to their own purposes — a generous move, and an effective one in securing an afterlife for his work. The imagery of fructification lends itself to the summer day outside:

> There is nothing final in the songs I write, not even the words, the rhythm and the melody. This is not an oversight; I would like to keep them growing, like a tree. They have a form, I hope; so does a tree. But it is not fixed and final. It must develop according to the time and place, it must adapt itself to soil and weather. In time, if not in place, a tree is always travelling. What kind of blue-print would allow for that? Cross out the 'blue'. Green things grow: call it a green-print.

I type 'Lord of the Dance' into YouTube and Carter's prophecy becomes reality — there are version of his song performed by Riverdance, Michael Flatley, The Dubliners and John McDermott. Carter might have been describing what was already happening to his songs rather than offering an open invite for them to be taken.[12]

Carter is not the poet I'm looking for; his lyrics are laid down too plaintively and in the traditional folk structures. His aim is to to delight through rhythms inherent in the language rather than musical melody and dense connotative imagery. As he writes about his song 'Judas and Mary': 'the melody is similar in style to one which keeps turning up in English folk song'. It is impossible to make words dance on the page whilst following set musical melodies.

Although his songs have massive airplay with Christian fellowships, particularly the Quakers, Carter has challenged traditional representations of Biblical figures and asked Christians to consider what they might learn from other religions. When the lyrics to his song 'Friday Morning' were published by the World Council of Churches in *Risk* magazine, their New York office received over two thousand letters of complaint:

> You can blame in on to Adam,
> You can blame it on to Eve,
> You can blame it on the apple,
> But that I can't believe.
> It was God that made the Devil
> And the Woman and the Man,
> And there wouldn't be an apple
> If it wasn't in the plan.
> It's God they ought to crucify
> Instead of you and me,
> I said to the carpenter
> A-hanging in the tree.

Carter looks back from his photograph with the stare of a man who never took the easy way through life. He has the countenance of the foreign correspondent who needs to understand the culture he's heading into — the differing shades of religious sanctimony — before he can consider offering an opinion on the state of affairs. Carter addresses his faith with this urgency: does he know enough to be sure he's in the right place? His religious thinking was no closed circle: he didn't believe in a devil, only the potential darkness in all of us. He didn't hold the core tenets of a doctrine before his more instinctive sense of what the story of Jesus actually *meant*.

It is the two words on Carter's stone that prove the most poignant, for me, of all the stones: given his cremation here there is a rich condensing of the whole life-death cycle into three syllables: MY CRADLE.

Stone for Sydney Carter displayed in a niche in the columbarium.

I walk around the cemetery for a while, trying to locate plot numbers and headstones with little success: graves have been plundered, unearthed, excavated. The cemetery was compulsorily purchased by Lambeth Council in 1965 but despite legal protections of the rights of current grave owners, the council undertook a maverick approach to bodily conservation. Under the cover of a protective veneer of language they used the perverse phrase 'lawn conversion' (not dissimilar, as a language trick, to the US government's use of 'transfer tubes' for 'body bags' during the Second Iraq War) to describe the process whereby they removed around 10,000 monuments and resold nearly 1,000 graves for reburials. This Ikea approach to the dead was ended by the Chancellor of the Diocese of Southwark in 1991.

There are also the elemental, degrading effects of time and weather: stone as subject to environmental change. As I follow the outside wall of the grounds a grave lies open on its side like an abandoned game of Fussball. I look inside: there's nothing to be seen that excites the sensationalist zombie fixation I grew up with. Loose earth, gentle roots, a beetle moving along in its black puffer jacket.

I could have walked hopelessly like this for hours but I take a chance on calling the number of someone I'm yet to meet: Colin Fenn of the Friends of West Norwood. He agrees to meet me at the gates in 10 minutes. A management consultant by profession, Colin brings the same focused sense of delivery to his projects relating to the cemetery. He has a way of bobbing about on his feet as he talks, as if all of the dead are pleading under his feet to mention them, reaching for his ankles — *me now, me*. Colin is on personal terms with many of the lives lived here. He knows more about the Norwood dead than anyone living: these are his charges. Knowledge of their back-stories is the alchemical ingredient for bringing them back to life. The histories Colin can tell is the opposite of Lambeth Council's illegal practice of 'lawn conservation'. The deeper we dig, downwards into the earth and backwards in time — into the loves, the lives, the chances taken and lost — the more we can live by what these lives can tell us. It's a form of biographical defibrillation; each fact, anecdote, joke, fires an electrical current back from the contraction of a heart to the ear of the listener. The unknown dead are all still in with a chance in this eternal lottery of ongoing legacies. And who really, amongst the buried, wants to be forgotten forever?

Colin drives me back to our starting point, the columbarium, and asks about my poets. He knows some of them already. While I've been digging into collections at the British Library and the Poetry Library, extracting phrases for engraving their stones with a watchmaker's precision, he's been lifting back headstones and cleaning their graves. Colin has a face animated by restless curiosity: if there's a connection to map out or a link to explore then he's happy. For the next two hours I shuffle as closely to his fast-moving heels as possible, the sheaf of notes and a copy of *Clotted Sun* under my arm. Meeting the dead is as quick-fire as a backstage pass at Glastonbury. Colin can introduce me to the now-famous 12 poets, but I can't rock up at their dressing rooms just when it suits me: I have to stay close to him.

We start with Sir William à Beckett (1806-1869) whose resting place is facing the columbarium (although his headstone has long been removed). à Beckett was born in London and after training to become a barrister migrated to Australia in his early 30s. His grave was cleared in the first sweep by Lambeth Council in the 1960s. I had a number of his words ready for his stone: CALM REPOSE,

HUMBLE GROUND, SECRET WORKINGS or ASPIRATING BREATH. There is a nice synchronicity given his missing headstone next to the path: UNKNOWN WAY.

Having come to England to see a doctor due to paralysis of a leg which then spread to his spine, he began to focus his efforts towards full-time writing. Yet his work has not just been dismissed but critiqued as doggerel. To his credit at least it was precocious doggerel. He wrote *The Siege of Dunbarton* in 1824 when was he was just 18 and at that point his ambitions seemed more contained. The 'advertisement' for the book says: *Written during a month's illness, printed for friends*. This realisation that he wouldn't be able to support his family through poetry alone — that first white light of comprehension — led him to give up one profession of text for another: law. He was much more successful with the legal interpretation of the written word. In 1852 he became the first Chief Justice of the Supreme Court of Victoria. Like an over-affectionate lapdog or a poisonous mosquito bite, his literary yearnings wouldn't leave him, and — to keep his ear to the ground for the alternating

thud of great poetry — he became editor of *Literary News* for a while. His involvement as a lawyer in the trials following the Eureka Stockade caused far more controversy than his poems ever would. This organised uprising of gold miners in Melbourne against the colonial authority of the UK had resulted in the deaths of at least 27 people and à Beckett was a judge over some of the court cases that followed, casting aspersion on the activists. à Beckett set a high moral standard of order and took his Christianity seriously. The political conservatism that scores through the pre-Romantic brick-building of his verse can also be seen in the title of an influential pamphlet he wrote in 1852 (under the declamatory pseudonym 'Colonus'): *Does the Discovery of Gold in Victoria Viewed in Relation to its Moral and Social Effects as Hitherto Developed Deserve to be Considered a National Blessing or a National Curse?*

His poem 'The First Goldrush at Melbourne' suffers badly from over-attention to stock phrases, conforming to the iambic tetrameter of *In Memoriam*, though at the expense of any rich and distinct formations of meaning. The poem is built like a wall on the page with each line adding its own bricks of received phrases. à Beckett layers thicker and thicker with the trowel of his morality:

> How it moves us--how it proves us--
> This bewildering tale of gold!
> How they glisten--how they listen--
> Eyes and ears when it is told!
> How it sets us all a-raving,
> How it sets us all a-craving,
> Thinking of what might be got,
> If we were but on the spot!
> Gone are many, some still linger,
> Waiting with unquiet heart,

> And few feel not itching finger,
> As they see the rest depart

After the death of his first wife Emily Hayley in 1841 he married her sister, Matilda Hayley. The 13 children that he fathered may well have included some from his first wife: there were red and green apples in the fruit bowl. Across the centuries it is tempting to think of the children of these eminent poets as still children, tying string to the legs of sparrows and itching in Victorian schoolwear. I picture him as a man who was successful and commanding in professional life, unable to understand how the same authority he projected in the realms of justice and order didn't generate the same success artistically. His daughter, Emma Minnie, became a successful painter and married another artist, Arthur Merric Boyd. In 1891 they both had a painting in the Royal Academy exhibition. The Boyd family became known for generating artists across the fields of painting, illustration, sculpture, pottery, ceramics, architecture, graphic design and music. Sir William à Beckett stands at the sideline, the efficient propeller of the bloodline: unread manuscripts ruffling under his armpits.

A left-leaning path takes us in the direction of Sir Thomas Noon Talfourd (1795-1854), a figure — and tomb — well known to Colin. Talfourd is the first-born of the 12 poets and bridges the gap between the 18th and 19th centuries. He was a Victorian poet, but one who had met those A-List Romantics Charles Lamb and S.T. Coleridge. The air starts to lighten between the morning sun and what looks like a pending storm. It is a relief to find Talfourd's radicalism offsetting the conservatism of à Beckett.

Talfourd was a Sergeant at the Bar and a Liberal MP for

Reading (he later asked Dickens to stand as second MP, though Dickens — saturated with offers at the time, from dinners to patronages — declined) and was elected as a Judge in 1849. 'I am really quite enraptured at his success,' Dickens wrote. The list of controversial issues he stood for is impressive: abolition of slavery,

Thomas Noon Talfourd. (Engraving by William Oakley
Burgess, 1840; after a painting by John Lucas.)

the bill to give divorced women custody of their children, universal male suffrage. His stone captures his clarity to find a new way against the wall of received opinion, a demand declared with conviction. SWEAR TO ME.

Talfourd was editor of *London Magazine* and a law reporter to *The Times*. He was, in the words of Peter Ackroyd, 'an example of early 19th-century catholicity of talent'. He was a friend of Dickens and Dickens loved him with him good reason: Talfourd was one of the first advocates in parliament for the Copyright Bill (he introduced the Bill in 1837 and it was passed into law in 1842). Dickens dedicated *The Pickwick Papers* to him in a language that weaves his affection for Talfourd's advocacy for protecting copyright with personal warmth for the friendship they'd formed. Dickens does this through an impressively delicate phrasing in which Talfourd's own efforts as a writer are deliberately conflated with praise on behalf of his endeavours protecting the rights of authors. Dickens frees himself from having to comment directly on Talfourd's literary gifts:

> To Mr Serjeant Talfourd, MP..
> My Dear Sir,
> If I had not enjoyed the happiness of your private friendship, I should still have dedicated this work to you, as a slight and most inadequate acknowledgment of the inestimable services you are rendering to the literature of your country, and of the lasting benefits you will confer upon the authors of this and succeeding generations, by securing to them and their descendants a permanent interest in the copyright of their works...
> Beside such tributes, any avowal of feeling from me, on the question to which you have devoted the combined advantages of your eloquence, character, and genius, would be powerless indeed. Nevertheless, in thus publicly expressing my deep and grateful sense of your efforts in behalf of English literature, and of those who devote themselves to the most precarious of all pursuits, I do but imperfect justice to my own strong feelings on the subject, if I do no service to you...
> Accept the dedication of this book, my dear Sir, as a mark of my warmest regard and esteem — as a memorial of the

most gratifying friendship I have ever contracted, and of some of the pleasantest hours I have ever spent — as a token of my fervent admiration of every fine quality of your head and heart — as an assurance of the truth and sincerity with which
I shall ever be,
My dear Sir,
Most faithfully and sincerely yours,
CHARLES DICKENS.
48, Doughty Street, September 27, 1837.

'The most precarious of all pursuits': on the cliff-face of literature — especially in comparison to my 12 poets — Dickens was well upholstered. Talfourd was one of those genuine friends that Dickens kept in mind as the social reward for meeting his writing deadlines. They were both frequenters of the Piazza Coffee House in Covent Garden and would meet on Saturday nights. There's an extant letter from Dickens to his friend and biographer John Forster, written in 1837 — at the time Dickens was working on *Pickwick* — which playfully suggests that Dickens will make it known to the public if Talfourd refuses to meet for dinner:

> We will be quite alone, and make no preparation. Persuade him; tell him how much he would delight me; how delighted I should be to relax for a few hours; and how much better I should work tomorrow morning, if I had such a prospect before me...Tell him in short that I will take no denial, and that if he doesn't come, I will state it in the Dedication and appeal to the Public

On one level Dickens' prolific writing output was driven by the early deadlines he set himself in order to keep his social assignations.

He would tuck himself under the cloak of night where the real observation of the city could happen. Claire Tomalin captures the excitement of the night for Dickens when he made 'night-time rambles through rough parts of London, mixing with the criminal classes, keeping an eye out for pretty street girls and drinking more than was good for [him]'.

Dickens' late-night play and his satire often went hand-in-hand. Talfourd couldn't pronounce his Rs and when Talfourd wasn't around Dickens was a keen imitator of this foible. There is a slight perversion to Dickens' mocking imitation of a man who was one of the staunchest advocates of the Copyright Bill.

Talfourd's play *Ion*, from which his stone SWEAR TO ME is taken, was performed at the Covent Garden Theatre to great acclaim. Written in blank verse, the action centres around the King of Argos, who declares himself a republican, steers his country towards abolishing the monarchy, and then commits suicide. The play was a massive success in London between 1836 and 1837, and was later revived and hailed as a masterpiece in America. It was the right play for the right time: William IV was ageing and soon to die, and Victoria was yet to couch the era with the metonymic charge of her name. The play captures the pre-Victorian nervousness of social change.

Talfourd's poetry, however, has never developed a readership. He was published by Dickens in 'Household Words', including a 'Sonnet to Robert Browning', which elicited a personal letter of thanks to the author from Browning himself. The poems read like the author's memory of Romantic verse. It is as if Talfourd's meeting with Coleridge (a radical genius of form through his creation of what are often called conversational poems such as 'This Lime-Tree Bower My Prison'[13]) had left an unshakeable pressure of attempting to create a 'great' poem through echoing the techniques of earlier poets. His poems were full of echoes at the expense of developing his own voice. Talfourd puts on the alternating end-rhymed iambic pentameter like a suit of iron that rusts as he tries to move with the flexible ease of the poets he admired.

V: To The Thames At Westminster
IN RECOLLECTION OF THE BANKS OF THE SAME
RIVER, AT CAVERSHAM, NEAR READING

With no cold admiration do I gaze
Upon thy pomp of waters, matchless stream!
But home-sick fancy kindles with the beam
That on thy lucid bosom faintly plays;
And glides delighted through thy crystal ways,
Till on her eye those wave-fed poplars gleam,
Beneath whose shade her first ethereal maze
She fashion'd; where she traced in clearest dream
Thy mirror'd course of wood-enshrined repose
Besprent with island haunts of spirits bright;
And widening on-till, at the vision's close,
Great London, only then a name of might
For childish thought to build on, proudly rose
A rock-throned city clad in heavenly light.

'Pomp of waters', 'matchless stream', 'lucid bosom', 'crystal ways', 'ethereal maze', 'mirror'd course', 'island haunts', 'heavenly light'. These phrases do not demand to be engraved into stone. They attempt to arrest the reader's interest through high-sounding gravitas but the meanings become incomprehensible or vague; 'pomp of waters' sounds like what it is: poetic liquid. This is poetry posing as poetry with a complete absence of startling syntax or rhythm. It is no surprise that Dickens — as little able to veer from his honest view as he was able to embellish that honest view through sophistry — avoided publicly praising Talfourd's poetry in his *Pickwick* dedication. For all his success as a playwright, Talfourd is not the forgotten poet I'm looking for.

Talfourd died of an apoplectic seizure whilst addressing the grand jury. Bombastic lungs and the gravitas of conviction expelled him into a Victorian puff of dust. Dickens was at his funeral. In her biography of Dickens Claire Tomalin fails to mention the passing of Talfourd and what this would have meant to Dickens as one of his oldest friends. Talfourd's life had captured so much of the drive and determination that Dickens admired. John Forster said of Dickens' affection for Talfourd that he 'had no friend he was more attached to'.

I follow Colin past the grave of Reuters, whose headstone carries a typo ("he needed a better sub-editor" Colin says), through a dense ground-level foliage of nettles. We stand next to his grave and I sense Dickens standing over the opened plot (Talfourd's father was down there too), gathering granules of dry mud in his ink-stained hands and scattering it down on the solid wood of the coffin. The dry knots of soil wrap like knuckles. The flat base of the gravestone lies before the rising pillar of Talfourd's monument. It is like a stone lamp-post, concealed amidst overgrowing bramble and nettle. Dickens is looking rakish in a long beard, a huge Victorian overcoat puffing his physique. He takes in a deep lungful of West Norwood air and reads from one of his own letters. It's impossible to improve on, he thinks, in way of dedication to one as great as Talfourd. 'To find a man,' he begins, 'So amiable a man, so gentle, so sweet-tempered, of such noble simplicity, so perfectly unspoiled by his labours and their rewards, is very rare indeed upon this earth.' He scatters another handful of granular soil across the stone slab.

Talfourd opens up a further link amongst the West Norwood dead: that of the novelist Anne Radcliffe (1764-1826). Radcliffe is a name I've heard lauded and, at times, reviled, but who is unquestionably significant in the development of the Gothic novel. "There is only a one percent chance," Colin says, " — but a

chance, that her bones are buried here". This sounds like a twist from Radcliffe's *The Mysteries of Udolpho*, a novel known for its kaleidoscopic, unseemly and dreamlike sequence of events. I know already from my research that she has no memorial here — so why her bones?

Colin explains. When the Bayswater burial ground in St George's Cemetery, Hanover Square, was emptied in a shocking series of exhumations to make way for a development of flats, an underground car park and a power station, many of the bodily remains came to West Norwood. These practices began in 1965 and offered a new regenerative model for body snatching: coffins were taken from the main burial ground and vaults to clear room for urban development. Relayed in transit, the dead were put into commute and moved to other cemeteries, including West Norwood. The restlessness of local councils runs in cycles and there was no long-term peace for these remains in Lambeth either as they undertook their own clearances during the 1980s. Many of these relocated memorials were bulldozed: "More recently a litter bin was set unintentionally on top of them — perhaps this is a subliminal message of the thought given to their disposal," Colin adds.

Anne Radcliffe had been buried in the vaults at St George's, but only one percent of those in the vaults were ever relocated. That one percent, along with the burials in the main grounds of St George's, would also have been reburied across three London Crematoria: St Mary-at-Hill, Enon Chapel and here at West Norwood. Colin has insider knowledge: the small number of vaults disturbed at St George's were at the furthest end of the underground building and Radcliffe was located in the middle. It is almost certain that she is still laid out beneath central London in the Anglican style.

Still, that night, I find myself pursuing Radcliffe, even if there is only a small chance of her being here — could she be my great lost poet? More famous as a novelist, many of her major novels have a significant subtitle: *Interspersed with some Pieces of Poetry*. These 'interspersions' — an interesting term in itself, suggesting the text-collage approach of later Modernist and Postmodernist writers — are of other poet's work as well as her own. Two of the poems — 'The Traveller' and 'The Pilgrim' — both published in *Udolpho*, were also previously published in journals.

The first biography of Radcliffe, 'Memoir of the Life and

Writings of Mrs Radcliffe', was written by Talfourd and included as a prefix to Radcliffe's *Gaston de Blondeville*, published in 1826, three years after the novelist's death. Radcliffe's fame had come much earlier with *Udolpho*, published in 1794. The novel was a popular success, securing the author an unheard-of advance of £500. Success came critically — and internationally — with Sade, Scott and later Poe praising her and claiming an influence. Jane Austen famously lampooned the book in *Northanger Abbey*, in which the heroine has a copy of the book given to her and the world is afterwards transformed into a mesmeric Gothic theatre.[14] Radcliffe's writing has not fared well in the 20th century, with Henry James critiquing *Udolpho* ('the everlasting castle in the Appenines') for its literary mistakes and the dissatisfying way in which Radcliffe attempts to tidy up so many of the supernatural strands which engaged her readers' interest to begin with.

This carelessness in her work brings to mind the poetry of Swinburne; like him she is capable of the most incredible descriptive writing, capturing vast swathes of the natural world in movement, yet she seemed to care little for the snip-and-snitch of the redrafting process. The power of her language — particularly of landscape — can be sublime (a term she used herself a lot, having been influenced by the thinking of Edmund Burke), but there is a sloppiness in her work too: as if the moment of creation is the main thing and the reader is best served by not having that moment cooled through later drafting. Perhaps Swinburne — and poetry generally — is better placed than the novel to exercise this licence (at least by geniuses in the field), with the novel's structuring of plot and character demanding a tighter weave.[15]

Terry Castle has listed some of *Udolpho*'s careless oversights, isolating her 'feeble ... characterisation' which is 'lacking in moral or intellectual *gravitas*' and 'full of absurdity and logical solecisms'. At one point in the novel Radcliffe forgets that all of her characters are supposed to be French and not English. 'Occasionally,' Castle says, 'Radcliffe makes bloopers of exquisite absurdity' such as when Emily, the main character, recognises the handwriting of her lover *engraved* into a stone (which brings to mind the stones I made for the 12 poets here, though I'd not thought of them as love letters) — a possibility that pushes the calligraphic potential of even a stonemason to suspension beyond disbelief. 'The general consensus among 20th century critics,' Castle says, 'is that *Udolpho* is 'bad' and fully deserving of Austen's satire. At times one feels that this is so.' And Castle, it should be observed, is a major advocate of her work.

But what about Radcliffe the poet? Radcliffe created a prescient kind of novel which was *Interspersed with some Pieces of Poetry*. This approach could be seen paving the way for the later experiments of James Joyce's *Ulysses*, in which the division between thought in poetry and poetry as thought — exemplified through the character of Stephen Dedalus — becomes impossible to separate. Radcliffe's use of 'interspersed' suggests a patchwork approach to writing that we have come to accept as a valid approach to literature through, for example, Walter Benjamin's epic collection of quotes about Paris, *The Arcades Project*.

Kenneth Goldsmith has written on this technique of appropriation in his polemic *Uncreative Writing*, arguing that before Benjamin's stroke of genius in presenting copied-out quotes from other books as his finished work, it 'had never occurred to anybody to grab somebody else's words and present them as their own.' Goldsmith makes the distinction between appropriation and collage, citing Pound's *Cantos* as a work that carefully selects other texts to create a harmoniously crafted new one. I would argue that Radcliffe's novels — interspersed with poetry — sits within the history of this approach to literature.[16]

Radcliffe's approach involves preceding each chapter with a quote from a poet (from Shakespeare or Milton, to many now much lesser known 18th century poets such as James Beattie, William Collins and James Thomson — as well as whole poems by the author herself), a trope which has become increasingly popular amongst novelists from the Victorian period to the current day. In addition — and more perversely, from the point of view of novel-writing — Radcliffe also includes snippets of poetry *within* the chapters themselves, often at moments in which the tension is building to its highest point. By doing this it is as though Radcliffe concedes that only the heightened emotion brought about through the condensed language of poetry can do justice to Emily's psychological torment in the castle of the evil Count Montoni:

> Leaving the splendour of extensive prospects, they now entered this narrow valley screened by
>
> Rocks on rocks piled high, as if by magic spell,
> Here scorch'd by lightnings, there with ivy green

Why struggle to find your own words for the sublime when poets have already done it? This quote, from James Beattie's 'The Minstrel', also suggests another reason for this technique. Radcliffe sourced poetry from popular poets of the day — as Beattie was — or from the classics, inducing in her reader the feel-good factor of recognising the words: a kind of literary spot-the-ball.

In the story of the novel Emily is also a poet, and Radcliffe presents this fact to us through many of the poems the character writes — fully formed in the moment — as if the complexities of thought can only be ironed out through the iron hooves of iambic tetrameter:

> ...anxious to escape from serious reflections, she now endeavoured to throw fanciful ideas into a rain, and concluded the hour with composing the following lines:
>
> Down, down a thousand fathom deep,
> Among the sounding seas I go;
> Play round the foot of ev'ry steep
> Whose cliffs above the ocean grow

There is another moment where Emily, encouraged by her father Monsieur St. Aubert, engages in a conversation around the prosody of the poem she has written, which she then goes on to read — the emotional romance becomes tied up with the unresolved poem. Standing here in West Norwood Cemetery, looking for a poet, with no one in sight above the open expanse of stone and grass, there is a familiarity to Emily's summoning of poetry:

> Emily laughed. 'Well, my dear sir,' said she, 'since you allow of this alliance, I may venture to own I have anticipated you; and almost dare venture to repeat some verses I made one evening in these very woods.'
>
> 'Nay' replied St. Aubert, 'dismiss the almost, and venture quite...'
>
> 'If it is strong enough to enchant your judgement, sir,' said Emily...'The lines go in a sort of tripping measure, which I thought might suit the subject well enough, but I

fear they are too irregular.'

THE GLOW-WORM

How pleasant is the green-wood's deep-matted shade
  On a mid-summer's eve, when the fresh rain is o'er;
When the yellow beams slope, and sparkle thro' the
    glade,
And swiftly in the thin air the light swallows soar!

Emily's concern about the irregularity of the lines was very much part of the poetic discourse of the time, with the freeing up of 18th century verse by poets like Christopher Smart paving the way for the breakthrough of Coleridge's more radical conversational poems.

Where is Radcliffe the poet in all of this? She is not, like Nabokov in *Pale Fire*, setting out to write poems which will then illuminate — or further mystify — her character. The poetry is an interspersion into the landscape of the novel for the sake of the poetry itself: the heightened language and ordering of sensation into form.

Should we see Emily's literary aspirations as another of her delusions, like the face that moves in the picture on the wall or the noises down the castle corridor in the haunted castle? The answer, I think, is no: Radcliffe was interested in literature as text, and wanted to keep the emotional pitch as high as possible — not necessarily through using each development as a way of furthering engagement with her characters — but through the tight weave of "the sublime" that poetry, suspense and landscape together can achieve. In a move that would be considered suicidal by many novelists, Radcliffe has Emily turn again and again to writing poetry until the novel itself becomes haunted by the formal rhythms of poetry.

The language that Radcliffe finds to bridge the change from one kind of text to another — from the novel to the poem — often becomes comical to follow. This is because Radcliffe is attempting to create a unified work from different texts that can't be reduced to a satisfactory meld. Here are some of the preambles Radcliffe uses to segue from Emily's story into the poem she's about to write, which, after a while, form a hilarious pastiche of jump-cuts: 'As Emily gazed upon one of the perilous bridges, with the cataract foaming beneath it, some images came to her mind which she afterwards combined in the following... '; '..she indulged her fancy in composing the following lines... '; '...she now endeavoured to throw her fanciful ideas into a train, and concluded the hour with composing the following lines... '; '...these awakened a train of images, which, since they abstracted her from a consideration of her own situation, she pursued for some time, and then arranged in the following lines; pleased to have discovered any innocent means, by which she could beguile an hour of misfortune'; 'It was after having witnessed a scene of the latter kind, that she arranged the following stanzas'; '... she indulged herself in imagining the pleasures of its short day, till she had composed the following stanzas'.

Despite the humour in the awkwardness of Emily's continual transitions into poetry, there is something significant about what Radcliffe felt unable to say about women writing at this time. Emily's poetry — which is clearly very important to her — is passed over trivially, as she indulges 'her fancy' with this 'innocent means' of passing the time. There is a cushion here, as if the male reader should not be threatened by this literary form of knitting. It is significant too that Radcliffe doesn't feel able to offer any insight into the female mind during its moment of creative inspiration — Emily's poems are lifted from her mind with no attempt to engage with the sensation of inspiration and process. In *Udolpho*, strangeness is all around Emily — borne of her delusions of the mind — but her writing is presented as something light and unthreatening. Her writing is her sanity and the reader should be reassured by this innocent, harmless pastime: she is no Chatterton, curled in a cold sweat in the white sheets of a bed in Hoxton, consumed by creative over-exhaustion.

Significantly, Radcliffe previously published two of the poems interspersed in *Udolpho* in journals, but her only poetry collection was a pirated edition of the poems from her novels which came out in 1816. This suggests that Radcliffe did consider them worthy poems. Yet after 1802 Radcliffe disappeared from society and chose to publish very little. There has been speculation that she was suffering from the evergreen condition of poets: mental illness. Talfourd wrote in his biography of her that her novel *Gaston de Blondeville* was 'laid aside, so disinclined had she become to publication'. Her willingness to publish poetry also fell into this apathetic vortex. Here I am surrounded by poets who desperately sought fame and here's Radcliffe — perhaps there, in the ground beneath the bin that Colin pointed out — pulling the veil from the glare that came with mass attention. She hid from what the 12 poets of West Norwood in some cases literally died for.

How does Radcliffe's poetry stand up on its own terms? Perhaps the best of Radcliffe's poems — later passed-off as Emily's — is 'Sonnet':

> Now the bat circles on the breeze of eve,
> That creeps, in shudd'ring sits, along the wave,
> And trembles 'mid the woods, and through the cave

Whose lonely sighs the wanderer deceive;
For oft, when melancholy charms his mind,
He thinks the Spirit of the rock he hears,
Nor listens, but with sweetly-thrilling fears,
To the low, mystic murmurs of the wind!
Now the bat circles, and the twilight dew
Falls silent round, and, o'er the mountain-cliff,
The gleaming wave and far-discover'd skiff,
Spreads the grey veil of soft, harmonious hue.
So falls o'er Grief the dew of pity's tear
Dimming her lonely visions of despair.

The poem is compact, tight and bound by the use of so many monosyllabic words. It follows the Shakespearean sonnet structure in rhyme and metrical construction; there is no attempt to push extant poetic forms. (Nothing unusual in that at this point in literary history — Leigh Hunt had made some initial rumbles, a scurrilous money-borrowing beaver in the dark tunnel towards free verse: Coleridge was the light-bearer). Yet there are some aspects of this poem which are difficult on the eye and ear, particularly the internal rhymes ('breeze of eve') and the irreconcilable jumps in sense produced by the pressurised restriction of the form ('That creeps' in the second line could be either the bat or the breeze). The poem is restricted from the more elastic expression that might come from freeing up the formal template Radcliffe is working in.

There is nothing in the poem which seizes the reader unconditionally through the imagery or demands them to view the world — or their understanding of poetry — in a new way . What the poem does — and does very well — is to create an *atmosphere*. Radcliffe wrote poems that could capture the mood induced from the world at distinct moments and in specific landscapes, which is why they were useful in her novels. I would suggest that Radcliffe came to be aware of this; that after publishing some of the poems separately, it dawned on her that any gift she had in poetry was in creating an emotional mood-board that could add texture to her novel. The poems promise to be lyric in their size and concern with a moment in time, but then become overly focused on narrative rather than condensed emotion. As such her poems neither fully lose the reader in the scenario nor take them to the higher levels of thought and emotion that lyric poetry can reach.

There are those — like Neal Cassady to the Beats — whose significance within literature is to inspire writers of greater gifts to create the work they might not have been able to do otherwise. Byron paid homage to Radcliffe's imagery of the city in his *Childe Harold's Pilgrimage*. Keats was so enamoured of her that he simply called her "Mother Radcliffe". It is her *prose* and not her poetry that moved them to this level of praise. Radcliffe's greatest poetry is undoubtedly in her descriptive prose passages:

> Vineyards stretched along the feet of the mountains, where the elegant villas of the Tuscan nobility frequently adorned the scene, and overlooked slopes clothed with groves of olives, mulberry, orange and lemon. The plain, to which these declined, was coloured with the riches of cultivation, whose mingled hues were mellowed into harmony by an Italian sun. Vines, their purple clusters blushing between the russet foliage, hung in luxuriant festoons from the branches of standard fig and cherry trees...

The building sense of rhythm here, developed through assonance — 'slopes clothed with groves of olives' — and the building of luxuriant fruits in succession, is the kind of writing that inspired Byron and Keats. Radcliffe's prose was free to follow a metrical pulse led by her passion for nature and an ability to tune itself to the inscape of the world around her. There is a hint of Hopkins' gift in this, yet there is a stronger sense of Swinburne's indeterminate excess and refusal to redraft. Radcliffe lost herself in the landscapes of her writing but had no interest in returning to prune the branches that had blossomed with the fruits of the work. Her writing is composed of a succession of moments of passion and inspiration — whether in her own words or those of others — and exists in a series of segments of poetry-and-prose loosely joined. We're invited to look at the real poetry — the prose — for the cuttings we'd like to take home.

It is a poem from *Udolpho* that offers itself as a prescient container for the possible exhumation of Radcliffe. This poem, by Frank Sayers, written in 1790, brings to mind that Radcliffe — like the woman described in the poem — might be without a burial plot:

> And shall no lay of death
> With pleasing murmur sooth
> Her parted soul?
> Shall no tear wet her grave?

With druidical sensitivity to the landscape, Colin maps out the plots of the dead poets, cuts through a section of overgrown graves and walks us towards the back wall of the cemetery along which poets Thomas Miller, John Overs and Edwin Milliken are buried. I have maps for each of them but arriving on their turf Colin explains that many of the headstones here have long been lifted. Miller, who I begin with, should be within Square 7, plot number 2921, but all around us is grass, sticks and consumer detritus that's drifted over from the housing estate beyond the boundary of the cemetery.

Thomas Miller (1807-1874) has been mythologised in children's anthologies such as *The Oxford Book of Children's Verse* as poetry's Dick Whittington. He was born in Lincolnshire to poor parents and worked as a ploughboy. He was extremely bookish and wrote poetry from an early age. Later he became a shoemaker's assistant and had — the story goes — a tyrannical boss who made his life unbearable. True to the moment of metamorphosis in fairy tales, he threw an iron instrument at his boss and moved to London.

It was here that Miller brought together his passions: he began to weave poems into baskets and sell them on the streets. This approach to making poems into physical objects precedes the concrete poet Ian Hamilton Finlay's radical textural sculptures by over a century. Unlike Finlay, however, Miller was no artist: he was a craftsmen — in his writing and his basket-making — and he struggled to push the boundaries of language or visual art. Whereas Finlay's inventions are numerous (not least of which was the 'one

Plan of Miller's grave in West Norwood Cemetery.

word poem' he invented) Miller's work moves like the *poor. old. tired. horse.* in the title of Finlay's seminal magazine. Miller's work is trite and pastoral:

> The day is past, the sun is set,
> And the white stars are in the sky;
> While the long grass with dew is wet,
> And through the air the bats now fly.
>
> The lambs have now lain down to sleep,
> The birds have long since sought their nests;
> The air is still; and dark, and deep
> On the hill the old wood rests.

As with many Victorian poets, Miller's poetry works by pushing used phrase-blocks around the established metrical frames that he works inside — 'sun is set', 'with dew is wet', 'sought their nests' — and there is none of the syntactical and syllabic dexterity that ignites the searingly original work of a poet like Hopkins. There is no attempt to weigh nature and God with his own distinct inscape. The poem is turned out like a well-functioning basket: pretty on the outside but empty.

We have met Dickens already at the graveside of Talfourd, and he appears again here. Dickens is the grand damselfly of Victorian writing — the ceaseless midge-swarm of lesser talents droned around him hoping for some refraction of his genius. His specular-light attracted Miller and he wrote to Dickens for patronage. Dickens declined, commenting to another friend by letter that 'he feared [Miller] had missed his true vocation'. Miller is the first of the poets to have no remaining headstone. Colin, with a boyish plunge into the undergrowth, pulls out a dead log — damp and riddled with lice — on which to place Miller's stone. We place it down in an opened slant of sunlight and realise the perfection: WOOD RESTS.

His neighbour, John Overs (1808-1844), is buried next door in square eight in what was known as the common ground. Colin tells me that there is evidence that a common grave would have cost just one guinea , opposed to the three of a standard private burial (in addition there were then funeral expenses and the rector's charges, including a fee for ringing the bell). Overs isn't simply missing a headstone; he was the only one of my poets never to have had one. I place his stone down. Although it may be little recompense for his lack of headstone or for his lack of afterlife readership, it provides an indication, at least, of his bodily and literary remains. His two words provide a riposte to his economy burial: AMPLE SOIL.

Overs had more success than Miller in catching the attention of Dickens. Overs had impressed Dickens with some songs he had sent, after which Dickens had visited him on occasion. Overs spent his evenings reading and writing, a pursuit that chimed well with Dickens' firmly-held beliefs that the self-educated man, given support, was a real possibility within a progressive society. When Overs fell ill with tuberculosis Dickens had helped him to find a physician. Overs had to give up work but his spirit — which again impressed Dickens — was one of endurance. Dickens wrote the introduction to Overs' book *Evenings of a Working Man* which — given Dickens' reluctance to offer patronage — was a huge triumph for Overs. Dickens wrote posthumously about him: 'He told me, how every small addition to his stock of knowledge made his Sunday walks the pleasanter. The hedge-flowers sweeter; every thing more full of interest and meaning to him... 'If I could only do a hard day's work', he said, 'how happy I should be!''

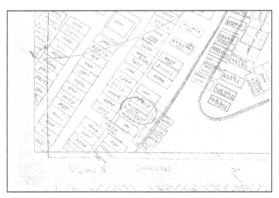

Plan of Overs' grave in West Norwood Cemetery.

Dickens, ever the polemicist for social change and an advocate for positive action amongst the working classes, turns the introduction to Overs' book into a mantra for education through the new programs of evening classes that were becoming available. 'Requiring only open eyes and ears, and six easy lessons of an hour each in a working town. Which will render them perfect for the rest of their lives'. This was one of only two introductions to other writers' books that Dickens composed in his life.

John Overs is coupled in memory with Samuel Laman Blanchard — another of the Norwood poets whose burial place I'll be arriving at soon — as they both died within a year of each other and Dickens worked towards raising money for both of their families. Yet they are the black and white of the same negative: Overs was in love with life and resented the illness that was slowly destroying him while Blanchard was a suicide who put an end to his life when he couldn't handle his depression any longer. West Norwood Cemetery took them both, the only distinction it made was along class lines, with Overs settling into the common ground here and Blanchard finding a place along the eastern wall alongside other known literary figures. The Norwood soil was ample enough for both of their bodies.

Next along in this triumvirate of the semi-remembered is Edwin Milliken (1839-1897). He was an editor of *Punch* and a humorist. In his lifetime he was much better known for his comic sketches than for his poems, with his character "Arry the Bombastic Cockney' becoming a big success. 'Arry was more caricature than character and reads now like an airbrushed Dickens out-take. The humour of Milliken's sketches resides in the Cockney dialogue of the literal-minded 'Arry who reads culture with an uncompromising matter-of-factness. Status games abound, as when 'Arry holidays at Stonehenge and meets a Druid whom he interprets as 'some old Arkylogical bloke'.

"Arry at Stonehenge', *Punch*, August 28th 1886.

Milliken wrote the poem 'Death and His Brother Sleep' which was famously quoted by Churchill when he believed parliament weren't taking Hitler's threat seriously:

Who is in charge of the clattering train?
The axles creak and the couplings strain,
and the pace is hot and the points are near,
and sleep hath deadened the driver's ear,
and the signals flash through the night in vain.
For death is in charge of the clattering train.

Auden might have had the rhythm of this poem in mind when he wrote *Night Mail*. Ironically, given Milliken's ability to couple together form and content so successfully — and his later airplay in Parliament via Churchill — he is the only one of the 12 poets never to have published a book of poems. I take a historiographical approach to selecting his two words and select: HUMAN NERVE. Milliken's face lives up to the words and, despite the ludic humour of 'Arry, he stares back with the austerity of a station master.

It starts to rain. We get into Colin's car and he points out a grave of significance in the distance. Raindrops fleck the windscreen. Colin pulls the visor of his red cap down in preparation for our next stop, the burial ground of the only female poet amongst the twelve, Menella Bute Smedley.

"You want to hear something surreal?" Colin asks as he closes the car door behind him and locks it with his keypad, "It's likely — or at least possible — that there's a part, if not all, of Laurence Sterne buried here". I laugh. I've spent the summer digging around for 12 unknown dead poets and now Colin says that an unequivocal genius could be spread out in particles beneath my feet. I think straight away of Laurence Sterne's timeline in *The Life and Opnions of Tristram Shandy, Gentleman* - used as a visual map of his digressive novel. I feel I'm on a similar course this summer.

Sterne, unlike the dog that crawls under the house to die, booked himself into a respectable inn on Bond Street when he knew his health was phasing-out towards death. He was buried at St George's but within hours his body was dug up by body snatchers. His corpse was sold to a professor of anatomy at Cambridge who recognised it as Sterne. In life Sterne referred to himself as Yorick: a man of infinite jest. When he was dug up, he was — like Yorick — recognised by his physical characteristics.[17]

In 1969, when St George's was being cleared, several skulls were dug up that showed signs of being anatomized. One in particular — a small skull — was similar in dimensions and proportions to a bust that had been executed of Sterne. The skull and other skeletal remains found next to it were taken to Sterne's old parish of St Michael's, Coxwold. The other remains went for burial at West Norwood. Later, however, Kenneth Monkman of the Laurence Sterne Trust could only say that 'they feel *reasonably sure*' (my italics, Colin's emphasis) that the skull and bones they'd taken out of London were in fact Sterne's. Which means, Colin says — the tale twisting into a smile — 'that West Norwood might have none, some, or all of Sterne's remains'. No one would have delighted in this more than the owner of the body.

The black page in *Tristram Shandy* comes to mind. Sterne uses this conceptual, visual trick to share his mourning for the death of his character Parson Yorick with the reader.

Colin, alert to as little as a dot of moisture transforming a field's humidity, stops where the gravestones end against an

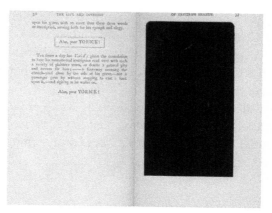

Black page in Laurence Stern's *Tristam Shandy* (1759-67).

impasse of rhododendron and nettle. He feigns throwing the stone of Menella Bute Smedley into the bushes. We've arrived at her plot but her grave has been overrun with bushes and brambles. Here's another of the poets without a visible headstone. Smedley has been lost to the undergrowth. There was no indication on the map that such a well-populated avenue of stones would now be replaced with bushes.

As with so many female Victorian poets, Smedley suffered illness all her life and couldn't live in the city, choosing instead to live in the seaside town of Tenby. Her father, The Reverend Edward Smedley, was also a poet and this literary condition spread virally through her family. In 1827 the family of five children moved to Dulwich, south of London: an established haven for poets. Her brother Frank, who was physically disabled, went on to become a popular novelist and her sister, E.A. Hart, was Smedley's collaborator in her books for children (and also a successful short story writer).

They were also cousins to Lewis Carroll and Menella translated a poem from German which influenced 'Jabberwocky'. Given the modest trickle of applause from her current, almost non-existent readership, it is this act of influence that proves to be her most visible contribution to the culture.

As well as writing poetry, Smedley was a novelist; the most evocatively titled of her novels being *Nina: a tale for the Twilight*. She also contributed to the social welfare issues of the time and — while

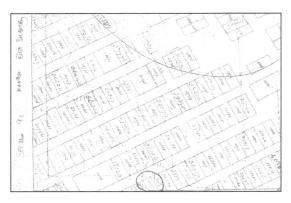

Plan of Smedley's grave in West Norwood Cemetery.

working as the Inspector for the Local Government Board for the education of girls in Pauper Schools — wrote the introduction to a series of reports called *Boarding Out and Pauper Schools*. Smedley writes of how these schools would often have as many as 1,500 children. The only language many of them had learnt was from the streets and their impoverished homes and their coarseness often came as a great shock to those trying to educate them, being seen as endemic of their innate corruption and lack of conscience which no amount of educating could correct. Smedley saw this differently, writing of 'these unhappy intruders [who] bring with them a knowledge of evil which it is painful to think of, and impossible to imagine in its full extent'. Smedley the poet is also present here as she evokes imagery that is both arresting and boldly metaphoric; she refuses to allow even her report writing to pale into cold, unfeeling chunks of text. She writes of how these schools have been forgotten 'during the plastic time of growth and education' and labels these massive pauper institutions as 'the Monster School system'. Here, at last, is a writer who cannot contain her own vitality for language and has an ability to conjoin disparate images into memorable new coinages — and this is even before I arrived at her poems.

As well as addressing childcare issues directly, Smedley was also a children's poet. She wrote *Poems Written for a Child* with her sister E.A. Hart, though, curiously, they declined to have their names printed in the book. The statement of authority is simply 'By TWO FRIENDS'. The copy I was handed at the British Library had its date of acquisition discreetly stamped in blue ink: British Museum 3 March 1868. It is hard to make a judgement on the quality of Smedley's poems here as it's not made clear which ones she wrote. The subjects of the poems cover many of the classic tropes of children's literature of this time and after: foxes, mermaids and birthdays. A poem called 'The Snow Dog' arrests my attention, calling forth Raymond Briggs' film of the same name which followed *The Snowman* and was first screened in 2012. On Christmas Eve we had sat down to watch this — Sarah, Pavel and I — with all the ghosts from the old stories tacking their fingers into the window's frost.

The penumbra of social reality is present in Smedley's poems for children too, as if — and here I am guessing which poems were written by Smedley — she couldn't quite pull herself from the pauper schools to write straightforward poetry of delight and wonder. 'The Sick Child' is written in the voice of a child singing to a bird and the facing illustration shows a child whose eyes are glazed as if possessed or in a state of high delirium. A woman and a man are carrying her in a chair though it's not clear where they are going. The poem — 'A Child's thought' — begins:

> Little beggar children, with your little ragged dresses,
> Does love atone for joys unknown by beautiful caresses?
> Or, do you live in happy homes as dear, perhaps, as this,
> And do you know that, come or go,
> You'll meet with eager kisses?

Smedley wasn't a poet who could put the knowledge she had of the world behind her to write poems that only operated beneath the melodic jewellery lid of 'verse'.

I make the announcement to Colin here, in the realisation that her headstone has been removed, that she is a contender for the most interesting — and talented — of the West Norwood poets. I've even brought some of her poems with me. Like me, Colin had not heard of her before. I tell him that the stone he's holding with the two words SUN UNSEEN comes from her poem 'April Showers', which is a close-up evocation of the shadows cast by the grass and flowers in summer. As with many of Smedley's poems there is the added interest of the poem not just being a lone meditation but also including a scene between two people: a conversation or an encounter. The world of her poems is enlivened with people agreeing, falling out and negotiating a shared view of society. This poem instantly pulls the reader in with the phrase 'He said... ' This leads to the man in the poem taking the hand of the narrator as she describes him as 'looking at me gravely, like a man / About to tell a secret'. Smedley makes an alluring invite into a strange world.

Smedley is skilled in raising the stakes of a poem from its opening. In terms of technique, 'April Shadows' alternates with end-rhymes that rest in couplets every fifth and sixth line: the movement of the shadows is arrested where these end-rhymes fall. Although there is nothing groundbreaking in this — or in the regular iambic pentameter — Smedley also uses an irregular indenting of her lines which is unusual for the time and suggests the sinuous play of light-in-movement that the poem evokes. Here is a poet who is completely in control of her techniques and can pack language down to arresting clusters of colour and detail. Although far from as radical — or as unique in rhythm and expression — as Hopkins, Smedley deserves her place in the anthologies of nature poetry:

> The great flags grow sedately. Down in glades
>   The riot and hurry of the rising spring
> Know them for rulers. All their emerald blades,
> Threaded with fires of gold, stand near the shades...
>   Each particular leaf,
>   Sharp as a spear and tender as a plume,
>   Lets fall its breadth of crystal gloom
>   To wave and flutter on the windy grass,
>   Or to lie still, if not a sigh should pass
> The lips of patient evening. None can name
>   The colour of these shadows, for they keep
> The tiny snow-stars and the cups of flame
> Safe in their shelter, softened, yet the same,
>   Like sights we love remembered in our sleep.
> On the fine limit of their lines of night,

> Grasses are gems, and lingering dewdrops sparks;
> They are not shadows, they are ambushed Light,
>   They are not lights, but they are lustrous darks,
> Films which no force can rend, no skill hath wrought,
> Impalpable and permanent as thought.

The chiasmus across light and dark creates a charge here as Smedley asserts that the shadows are not shadows but 'ambushed Light' and then immediately retracts this in the following line: 'They are not lights, but they are lustrous darks'. Smedley doesn't shy from complexity: the world is intricate and she grasps for the language to do justice to it. The lyrical flow of the poem — its suppleness — captures the moment's impact upon the eye and the ear; the sinuous lineation of the lines and the five- or six-line sentences with their alternating end-rhymes bring the form and content into union. There is also the triumph of the imagery, the technique that no poet can learn through guidebooks on the craft. Smedley is ambitious, reaching towards Hopkins' inscape, using the vessel of the poem, as he does, to capture the instress and allow it to travel towards the reader in perpetuity. The connections and overlays of the disparate movements and objects of the world create imagery of fascinating detail, especially around something as amorphous as the colours of shadows: 'The tint snow-stars and the cups of flame'. Many poets might have settled just for 'snow-stars' here but the addition of the adjective "tint" shows Smedley fine-tuning language to create imagery which is unique and fitting to the moment she is attempting to capture. The image becomes one of bright and dark at the same time.

　　'April Shadows' is the perfect poem for West Norwood today: light and shadow weave across the rhododendrons covering the ground above where she is buried. Colin is pulling the bushes back, trying to get inside, but there's no hope of bringing Menella out into the sun and her deserved readership: at least not without shears and a rewrite of the Leavisite canon.

The collection that 'April Shadows' comes from, *Poems* (1868), also contains her poem 'A Contrast'. This poem is a significant contribution to women's literature of the period and should be discussed alongside Christina Rossetti's 'Goblin Market'. [18] Smedley raises many of the concerns that Rossetti raises, especially around woman's relationship to male societal dominance, and whether

> To make a helpmeet for a man
> Is woman's perfectest of works

are values that should go unquestioned. The poem is not as original in technique as 'Goblin Market' and there are stylistic problems. Smedley is far too drawn to simplistic generalisations ('the mothers cry') and to trite synecdoches around nature ('O little garden in the wood, / So full of safe and tender bloom!') and there is an overly moralistic intervention from the author ('God guide the footsteps') that leaves the work short of Rossetti's (and Dickinson's) cryptic lyrics.

Although without the charged allegorical textures of Rossetti's poem, 'A Contrast' is fascinating for its reversal of the conventional sexual experience of the bride and groom on entering marriage. Although the poem is full of vague images around gardens and virginity and is technically restrained through its sustained octosyllabics that thud in an unchanging A-B-B-A rhyme scheme, a remarkable moment takes place in Smedley's poem. The woman in the poem marries a man who has 'a tedious modern sneer' and on saying 'Yes' to him she finds that 'A word divides her from her past'. Smedley describes a marriage that falls into place without passion. The woman, however, decides to confess to her new husband that she had thought of other men before their marriage. Fascinatingly, there seems to be no purpose to this confession other than attempting to shake the status quo and to make the man see her as a woman defined by her own desires:

> 'You must not frown. I have a shame,
>   A something which you ought to know;
>   I should have told it long ago, -
> You will forgive, though you must not blame:
>
> 'Before you wooed me I was sought, -
>   I know not why. I told you true,
>   I never cared for man but you,
> Yet once I wavered in my thought.
>
> And I was vain, as girls are vain,
>   But, O! it was fault to play
>   With one true spirit for a day!
> I could not do the deed again.'

Although the language — and the allegorical conceit — is far from as interesting as 'Goblin Market', the fact that the woman confesses a sin, *just for the sake of it*, is fascinating in the context of women's poetry at this time. The man is deliberately made to needlessly suffer:

> 'So I, most confident of men,
>   Was not the first!' She shook her head;
>   For, 'O! it was a fault!' she said,
> And 'I have wept for it since then.'

The poem reaches a compact and memorable moment when the relationship seems likely to fail:

> White soul, with such a fault! He thinks,
> Is, then, the darker soul more strong
> Because it does the deeper wrong?
> Because it fails? Because it sinks?

This confession actually saves their relationship as the man learns 'to think more truly of his kind'. Against the oppression of a one-sided relationship the woman carves out an openness, a healthy space between them in which equal dialogue might take place. A year later she reminds him of their conversation: "You never check her with that tone / Of fond contempt you gave your bride" and:

> He looks at her with reverent eyes,
> He clasps her with a generous shame;
> 'There was a revelation came
> From your angelic fault!' he cries

Smedley is a poet to be revisited. Poems of curious relationships and situations shed fresh light on much of the static of Victorian poetry. Her poem 'Cavour', for example, about the Italian Statesmen who was influential in uniting Italy but died before seeing it happen could be argued as a precursor for Carol Ann Duffy's *The World's Wife* (which falls far short of the psychological perspicuity that is possible in the dramatic monologue as exemplified in the work of Browning). Smedley is again interested in the female perspective. The poem opens with a woman running, shouting "Cavour is dead" and she then goes on to tell the narrator that she is the wife of the ceased statesman. The poem gains its interest and impetus from this quick, mysterious exchange. The woman, although in mourning, assumes her place at Cavour's throne with alacrity:

> I think I shall not die upon his grave,
> But, when I take my place, and wear my crown,
> And the world wonders, men shall stoop to read,
> Upon the topmost step of my great throne,
> An epitaph — "Here lies Cavour; a man
> Who built the throne of Italy, and died".

My place, *my* crown: the wife is in full acceptance of his death and assumes the legacy of power with an instinctive grace and authority.

Not all of Smedley's poems are as triumphant. She often employs the ballad without charging the language with any renewed sense of vitality. She also wrote what she called 'Dramatic Poems'. Smedley was obviously aware of the revolution in the dramatic monologue although this increase in the number of voices automatically reduces the propensity for psychological penetration. Smedley is at her worst in her poems of direct political engagement, for example 'Our Welcome to Garibaldi', which suffers from that immediate death of all poems: patriotism ('they sword sprang never from its sheath / Except to cleave a chain'). 'On the Death of Prince Albert' fails — as so many patriotic poems do — for telling the reader what they *should* already know. All of the colour and movement that the reader is offered in 'April Shadows' is lost here:

> Out of the tomb the world's hope went of old,
> > While angels shone around, Force shrank
> > away,
> And weeping love eternally consoled,

Went back to labour in the light of day

Smedley's work is included in the Victorian women's anthology *Poets and the Poetry of the Century*, which suggests how highly esteemed she was in her lifetime. Smedley is represented by seven poems; Emily Bronte by just six.

I tell Colin as we stand against the rhododendrons that this is West Norwood's greatest poet, though I have to be honest too: she falls short of the immense poet I've been looking for. Inconsistency lets her down, as does her facility in perpetuating the received patriotic thought of the time. But at her best, she was an incredibly gifted writer. As the introduction to her poems in the *Poets and the Poetry of the Century* reads: 'If the poet was born and not made, Miss Smedley was by nature a poet'. The months of journeying into the grounds and poems of the dead feels vindicated.

I lay her stone on the fringe of the bushes. It reads as a warning to the aspirations of immortality in every poet, especially that of the Victorian woman.

Colin moves us around the path, a kind of South Circular of stone. As we approach The Ship's Path a vista opens out across the cemetery, and Colin, checking my list of poets, points towards a flat capped table-length obelisk barely visible above the ground. Here is the cemetery's most famous literary name, Theodore Watts-Dunton (1832-1914). His legacy resides in his friendship with Swinburne. In 1879, fearing for his friend Algernon Swinburne's life, he asked the younger poet to move in with him: Swinburne stayed for 30 years.

The portrait of Watts-Dunton at this time could have been lifted from the wood figures of a 1970s children's program like *Trumpton*; rosewood-cheeks inflame his face as a handlebar moustache droops over his mouth. His legacy as a friend and supporter to the artists he knew is without question and the stone I lay down on the verge of the kerb opposite the Ship's Path — LOVE'S BREATH — reflects that.

Theodore Watts-Dunton. (Painting by Helen Bramwell Norris, 1902.)

Although most famous as the person who saved Swinburne from an inevitable early death, Watts-Dunton also had his own spate of literary success with his novel *Aylwin*, published in 1899. The novel is based on Watts-Dunton's obsession with gypsy girls and is about a boy who becomes disabled after an accident climbing the rocks along the coast. Unlike the novels of Hardy (the last of which, *Jude the Obscure*, had been written in 1895 — its harsh critical reaction turned Hardy to writing poetry for the rest of his life) Watts-Dunton's writing suffers from a necessity to spell out the consciousness of his main character in wearying detail. The first person address gives the reader no room to reimagine the character's complex psychology:

> From that moment I had become a changed being, solitary and sometimes morose. I would come and sit staring at the ocean, meditating on tilings in general, but chiefly on things connected with cripples, asking myself, as now, whether life would be bearable on crutches.

'On things connected with cripples' — as writing this is simultaneously vague and overly descriptive. Authorial distance is lacking. That the book had an impact at the time is beyond doubt: one day in June I felt the legacy in my hands. After sharing an Indian meal on Renshaw Street in Liverpool, I walk with my mum and brother in to the antique dealers 69a, my favourite shop in the city. *Antique* here means what we — in our family — once owned in our lifetimes. There is the cream phone we had at home and on which I made the first dial-in to my identity. There are the Beatles' albums that we owned too — *Rubber Soul, Revolver, Abbey Road* — the albums of my mum's youth that, if she still had in good condition, could be used to hatch a retirement plan. At the back of the shop, in the vitrine, is a box of snooker balls glinting in ebony primaries. My brother, an ex-professional of the baize, remembers with me the clinked colliding of coloured planets across the table we had at home.

I lose myself in the books at the back of the shop; stock from the 1970s including *How to Deal with Sex Addiction* sit alongside recovered editions of Dickens. I scan the shelves and the gilt lettering of a leather-bound pocket-size edition catches my eye: *Aylwin*. If one of my starting points was to think of Victorian writing as parallel to the cobbled streets we still walk then here's evidence of Watts-Dunton's place, however small, in the corpus of above-ground literature. It's a third edition from 1906 (the fact of being reprinted on two successive occasions gives evidence to its success). I buy the book: its legacy still active, at least in my cultural experience. It fits tight in my pocket as we walk into The Dispensary, the Victorian pub next door.

Aylwin is listed in *The Oxford Chronology of English Literature*, as is Watts-Dunton's poetry collection *The Coming of Love and Other Poems*, published the year before in 1898. On picking up a copy of this book the immediate impact is of the cover's green-and-gold cover. The title page has one of the cleanest examples of a trade deboss I've seen; the alternating red-and-black text calls forward the designs of Soviet constructivism. This excitement of promised modernity soon disperses on opening the book. At the back there's an advert for another of Watts-Dunton's collections, *Jubilee Greetings at Spithead to the Men of Greater Britain*, which includes a whole host of quotes celebrating the author's patriotic gravitas: 'His verses breathe the spirit of fraternity among all the peoples of the Empire' — *The Times*; 'The Jubilee has not gone by without at least one poetical commemoration of dignity and merit. It has genuine emotion and living imagery' — *Bookman*; 'The poem is a noble one' — *Literary World*; 'Spirited and patriotic' — *The Guardian*; 'Fine verses in an exalted vein of Imperial patriotism' — *St. James's Gazette*. Despite the praise, *Jubilee Greetings* has sunk without trace, appearing neither in bibliographies of the poetry of the time nor in reference to the poet himself. Patriotic poetry is met with the shield of praise for a short time only. After researching Watts-Dunton I quickly became doubtful that this is a poet who can hold the complexities of a changing world and find language for the non-entrenched viewpoint.

Modern poetry collections tend to be between 60 and 80 pages. Although this has become a prize-winning convention it was far from the case in the 19th century and *The Coming of Love* runs to a titanic 136 pages.[19] I take a breath before looking at the poems. The first two poems alone run for 83 pages. The reading experience immediately grates with its questionable truncation of the word 'assuage':

> If heaven's bright halls are very far from sea,
> I dread a pang the angels could not 'suage

I bring to mind that other measure I set for seeing through the poets of occasion and singsong to the powerful and original: whether or not the metrical template of the poem is stretched through the vitality of language and whether the confidence of voice or originality of syntax can push against the syllable count of received poetic form. The grating and unappealing ''suage' is used here to ensure the line sits down and heels to the bumping melody of the iambic pentameter. In compromising between sense and convention Watts-Dunton comes down clunkily on the latter. Incredible feats can be performed within tight established forms, but ''sauge' isn't one of them.

As the poem unfolds it's clear that Watts-Dunton's view of his work has a worthy sense of *rightness* in the things he celebrates — England, the navy, Empire — and that this sense of what is right in the world is bound with the poetic techniques that he also felt were unquestionably *right*. End-rhymes are used like rivets in ships of trade, with very little openness to the possibility that rhyme can take place at *any* point throughout a poem. One senses that for Watts-Dunton to question the tenets of English poetry would also have been to question England itself. It's tempting to see his befriending of Swinburne as similar to Gladstone's project to save prostitutes: he could save the fallen eccentric and save England at the same time. By inviting Swinburne into his home at The Pines, the streets of London, and English poetry would be simultaneously cleansed. Watts-Dunton's poetry represents the clean, organised streetplan of an England that exists as an ideal in a metrical Albion of the mind.

In addition to this marking out of the straightforward grid-card of regularised cadence (every one of the 260 pages is in iambic pentameter) his poems are stocked with staid and received expressions: 'the magic wonders of the world'; 'Like fiery snakes'; 'Must flee like doves away'. There are a few poems I'm drawn to simply because of the allure of their titles; 'A Talk on Waterloo Bridge' for the literary legacy that precedes it, but also because I see the bridge every day from my window at work. I find a thread of interest in the sense of time collapsing across the century, yet the regulated brickwork of Watts-Dunton's poem immediately rebuilds the historic poetic disparity.

Watts-Dunton is a poet without self-awareness who harks back to unquestioned forms and looks upwards to the imagined Gods of inspiration. One poem begins bombastically: 'Hear us, ye winds!' The poet's voice is muffled with echoes of his idea of the tempests exhaled by the Romantics. He often uses the technique of parataxis — the juxtaposition of clauses without conjunction — to ensure he keeps to the tally-count of syllables, but he does this at the expense of a language that is vibrant and natural: 'I see the pine like her in golden story' ('Coleridge'). His imagery is very often weak and contrived, for example when talking of art and poetry combining: 'The painter's wizard-wand, the poet's spell' ('In A Graveyard'). It is no surprise to find in Watts-Dunton's book of prosody *Poetry and the Renascence of Wonder* a contempt for the free verse of Whitman (a revolutionary poet in the history of free verse and also a poet who was said to have admired Watts-Dunton's lodger, Swinburne) through the coupling of open thought and expression with ideas of nationhood:

> To discuss the metrical movements of the most famous innovator in this line, Walt Whitman, has become positively painful, especially to those who sympathise with the liberal and generous views these innovations embody; but it would be uncandid to shrink from saying that the endeavour to imitate this movement of our sublime English Bible in poems where the jargon of the slums is mixed up with Bible phraseology and bad Spanish and worse French finds it hard to condone.

The idea of correct form is bound with a sense of Englishness and with it English 'authority'. Whitman is a guttersnipe, usurping the majesty of the English language with his corruptions from the American 'slums'.

Perhaps the most effective way to consider the distance between Watts-Dunton's work and that of the emerging Modernism is to compare his work to his contemporary, Arthur Symons. Symons was an innovator and originator and — despite his absence from the anthologies — is one of the most important poets of this period. Susan Howe describes him in one of her poems as 'of fringe prominence / in the aesthetic Nineties' yet his legacy has proved much bigger than his status at the time would have suggested. He bridged the line between the imagistic potential of Symbolism and the more precise if fragmented possibilities of Modernism. Symons' collection *London Nights* was published three years before Watts-Dunton's *The Coming of Love and Other Poems*, but foreshadows the next epoch of modern poetry that Watts-Dunton was entrenched against. Here's Symon's 'Autumn Twilight' in full:

> The long September evening dies
> In mist along the fields and lanes;
> Only a few faint stars surprise
> The lingering twilight as it wanes.
>
> Night creeps across the darkening vale;
> On the horizon tree by tree
> Fades into shadowy skies as pale
> As moonlight on a shadowy sea.
>
> And, down the mist-enfolded lanes,
> Grown pensive now with evening,
> See, lingering as the twilight wanes,
> Lover with lover wandering.

It was Symons who inspired Yeats to read the French Symbolists and — significantly in the case of the poem above here — inspired Eliot to read Laforgue. The opening lines of this poem are clearly echoed in the opening of Eliot's 'Prelude':

> The winter evening settles down
> With smells of steaks in passageways.
> Six o'clock.
> The burnt-out ends of smoky days.

Eliot had read of Symons' *The Symbolist Movement in Literature* and wrote that it was a 'revelation', offering, in poetry, 'an introduction to wholly new feelings'. In an issue of *The Criterion*, Eliot's own magazine, he wrote:

> I myself owe Mr Symons a great debt: but for having read his book, I should not, in the year 1908, have heard Laforgue or Rimbaud; I should probably not have begun to read Verlaine; and but for reading Verlaine, I should not have heard of Corbiere. So the Symons book is one of those which have affected the course of my life.

Symons looked back at different poetic traditions and unlike Watts-Dunton, looked sidewise to contemporaries in other countries, both assimilating and discussing new possibilities for the future of English poetry. Ezra Pound was impressed with him too, writing in 1911 that 'the Gods in whom he found his sanity were Plato, Longinus, Dante, Spinoza, Pater and Symons'. Symons features amongst an international cast. I would argue that his influence can also be seen in Pound's poetry. Symons' poem 'Morbidezza', from his earlier collection *Silhouettes* (1892), begins:

> White girl, your flesh is lilies,

Under a frozen moon,
So still is
The rapture of your swoon
Of whiteness, snow or lilies.

As with the Eliot poem above, there is a clear influence on Pound's
'A Girl' from his collection *Lustra*, published in 1916:

Tree you are,
Moss you are,
You are violets with wind above them.
A child — so high — you are.
And all this is folly to the world.

Pound takes his poem to the logical next step of relaxing the end-
rhymes, yet the 'rapture' of a young girl, depicted through the
metamorphosis of her flesh to an aspect of nature — lilies in Symons'
poem, a tree in Pound's — shows a clear influence on the later
poet.[20]

Symons wrote: 'To be modern in poetry, to represent really
oneself and one's surroundings, the world as it is today, to be modern
and yet poetical, is, perhaps, the most difficult, as it is certainly the
most interesting, of all artistic achievements'. He wrote of the chaos
of the city, its prostitutes, drinkers and drug-takers and yet did all
this while retaining a lyrical beauty within his work. 'I think', he
said, 'that might be the test of poetry which professes to be modern:
its capacity for dealing with London, with what one sees or might
see there'. Despite Watts-Dunton's role as a critic and his extended
writing about poetry, there was no sense in which he believed
that poetic form might be required to change to do justice to new
experiences and that aspects of grime and degradation had a place

in modern poetry. To be modern — as Baudelaire and Rimbaud had suggested before — was to embrace filth. It is one of the great losses to literature that after his mental collapse in 1908 Symons wrote almost no poetry until his death 30 years later.

Colin and I walk forwards towards another broken poet: Samuel Laman Blanchard (1804-1845). I discovered him amongst the dead Norwood poets rather late in my research and as a result I have no plot reference for him. Even his name is unclear: according to the records his birth name, Edward Laman Blanchard, was engraved on the headstone — which has now disappeared — and it also carried the incorrect birth date of 1803. These factual misnomers are suggestive of a ghost-in-life, a man not quite present in name and identity. He committed suicide with a razor after falling into a depression following his wife's early death. Blanchard was working as a proof-reader at this stage but his strength was already broken from overwork and grief. Suicides are restless; I see them as cyclical Os: no X marks their spot.

As I was researching Blanchard's extant works at the British Library, I stumbled into an unexpected fact: he was also a stalking revenant of cemeteries. In 1843 his book *The Cemetery at Kensal Green: the grounds & monuments* was published. There was always something destined-for-the-grave about Blanchard and I make a note of his cemetery book for the Kensal Green stage of my journey through the Magnificent Seven.

Blanchard was born in Great Yarmouth and then educated at St Olave's School in Southwark. His great friend — the playwright and wit Douglas Jerrold — lies under the burnished magnificence of his gravestone just yards from where Colin and I scratch around looking for an accurate and suitable spot to place Blanchard's stone.

The two friends, in their youth, were great adventurers of the mind: they had pledged to fight alongside Byron in Greece and then to embark on a theatrical career (Blanchard achieved neither and was more of an emergent Victorian than a Romantic hero). Blanchard worked for a number of magazines including *Monthly Magazine* (offering poetry and verse), *The Constitutional*, *The Examiner* and *Ainsworth's Magazine*.

Colin weighs up the size of the plot, angles his arms across the cemetery like an experienced golfer about to pitch across the Styx towards Hades. Colin points towards a spot on the ground: as good a place as any to mark Blanchard's plot. The ONE DAY of his stone captures the poet's restlessness but also his wish for afterlife unity with his wife. We tuck the stone against the border of the cemetery wall and Colin trails fronds of pink petals in front of it. A bouquet of remembrance.

Blanchard was only 25 when his collection *Lyric Offerings* was published. The title recalls Wordsworth and Coleridge's *Lyrical Ballads* and, as such, is characterised by its nostalgic sense of poetry.

Daniel Maclise's skectch of a literary gathering in 1844.
Blanchard is sitting third from left.

It is one of his comic poems that remains the most quotable. I read it out loud to Colin here, in this quiet corner of the cemetery — a few yards from the legendary wit of Jerrold and the conviviality of Watts-Dunton — and we both find ourselves laughing out loud in response to a poem (enough to rustle a crow behind us) from the poet who committed suicide at his home, in Lambeth, aged 42:

from 'The Art of Book-Keeping':

A circulating library
  is mine — my birds are flown;
There's one odd volume left to be
  Like all the rest, a-lone.
I, of my Spenser quite bereft,
  Last winter sore was shaken;
Of Lamb I've but a quarter left,
  Nor could I save my Bacon.

Alongside Blanchard is Henry Dawson Lowry (1869-1906). His stone is still intact in a kind of mottled salmon-pink simply etched with Gothic text. Colin shares my excitement: he lives for classic Victoriana like this. Lowry was four years younger than Blanchard when he died and left behind an illustrious catalogue of enticing book titles, particularly for his novels: *Wreckers and Methodists, and other stories* (1893); *Women's Tragedies* (1895); *A Man of Moods* (1896) and *The Happy Exile* (1908). He also wrote for the magazines *The Ludgate* (of which he was also the editor) and *The Chap-Book*. His work is currently kept in print by the British Library and has benefited from the ruthless egalitarianism of OCR technology that can turn poetry into data for cheap reprinting.[21]

Lowry, then, like many almost-forgotten writers has found himself in the nebulous position of being still 'in print' though largely unread — especially by those publishing him, if the typos and lack of formatting in the books is anything to go by. His fiction is often written in a cloying Biblical tone and wrought with such intensity that the prose refuses to flex. Occasionally, though, the dreadnought grey of the prose breaks blue water with an arresting image. His story 'The Last Pagan' is so tense that the serifs could be snapped by hand, but there is an occasional force to the writing too and an interesting fusing of images around sun, worm and stone:

> The altars were cold. The priests, already regarding themselves as members of an order long established in the land, had seized upon the holy places and proclaimed themselves the interpreters of their mysteries: so that if water healed, or a sick child recovered strength when it had been passed at sunrise through the holed stone, the people no longer gave thanks to the old gods, who

had been wont to confer their mercies by these means throughout all the centuries which had been before the coming of the priests from overseas. Even the senseless dead might no longer get the purification of flame. There was need that their miserable bodies should be kept whole, and so they were laid in graves digged in the earth, where the unclean worm might prey on them; and the grey priests muttered prayers above, and sprinkled water they themselves had sanctified by virtue of their words.

These cold altars, the holed stone, the senseless dead and the unclean worm all press sharply into the mind. Yet Lowry would have been much more successful as a writer if he had limbered a little at his lectern. Writing is about learning how to perform all the techniques well and then learning to forget them a little — at least enough to weave the kind of distinct associations that is unique to the individual talent.

There is a Dulwich connection with Lowry too. I find this link in the introduction to *The Happy Exile*, a kind of anti-London polemic in which a series of 'papers' are found in the drawer of a man that document his journeys taken out of the 'prison' of London and into the country. Two of the papers, Lowry reflects, must have been written after the man returned to London — the point at which he would have lost his happiness: 'I can fancy they were produced after he had slowed himself to become a prisoner in London. The married man must have his occasional reflections, and he has surrendered many things in return for the privilege of his pretty house at Dulwich'.

Lowry wrote a book of poems called *The Hundred Widows*

which was published in 1904. It follows an interesting near-Modernist structure with each poem being numbered and positioned with plenty of white space around it (there is no real white space on the Victorian page, off-white, beige and cream predominate) as if to conceptually suggest a real window through to the thoughts, or inner life, of the poet. The poems however are late Victorian and fit within the tradition of the ballad rather than the new possibilities for poetry which were being suggested at this time:

> Stars shine softly down in the West
>   And your lost youth comes to find you,
> With word of the girl that you loved the best
>   In the days you have left behind you
>
> Sleep comes easily there in the West
>   And the dawn is loth to wake you;
> So take your fill of the boon of rest,
>   Happy as dreams can make you.

Ezra Pound's first collection, *A Lume Spento*, was self-published four years later and a quick comparison with almost any section of any poem is enough to show how Lowry's work, however well-made, suggests no possibilities for significant use to the poets of the future. The opening of Pound's 'Cino' should be enough to make the point, with its unexpected colloquial exclamation and its lines led by a natural inflection of speech rather than the tapping finger:

> Bah! I have sung women in three cities,
> But it is all the same;
> And I will sing of the sun.

Lowry is not lacking in an ear for straightforward formal verse but as with his prose he favours an over-bearing use of received phrases like 'boon of rest' rather than with any distinct conjunctions of words. Pound groups words together to create units of rhythm that surprise and add supple complexity to the meaning and flow of his poems. It was no doubt poets like Lowry, steeped in a post-Tennysonian poetic framework, that Pound had in mind when talking of arriving

in London with the intention of aiming to '(to break the pentameter, that was the first heave)' (Canto 81). Lowry is not my original. I place his poem at the base of his headstone: DAY LINGERS. At the top edge of the stone two ladybirds are copulating.

The late afternoon sun is fading and there is still John Yarrow to find. Tonight is the opening of *Curious* and Colin has to leave, wash, dress and be ready for the public. When I was researching the poets I came across John Yarrow online — the wrong John Yarrow: 'A graduate of The UK School of Toastmasters, [he] has the experience and qualifications to make him the ultimate choice to preside over your wedding, corporate or private function'. Successful identification followed and the real John Yarrow's grave should be easy for me to spot due to a photograph of his headstone that I discovered on www.findagrave.com. The headstone was shot against a clear winter backlight with a stripped tree cracking the white sky. The headstone itself slightly askew in the earth. John Yarrow: 1818-1898. POET ORATOR AND PAINTER.

I rack my brains for examples of successful poets-cum-orators and get as far as John Donne. Shakespeare could certainly write great oratory. The history of oratory and poetry goes back to the Greeks and even then the distinction between the mechanics of rhetoric and the function of poetry has been a fraught one.

Rhetoric was a part of the formal education offered to children up until the end of the 19th century and I can't help feeling that the West Norwood poets who failed most, à Beckett, Talfourd and here — Yarrow — are the ones who failed to make the distinction between suppleness of poetic language and rhetoric. They didn't see that poetry turns to clods of iron if used as a language device for argument or orchestration of a viewpoint. As Yeats declared (a poet himself praised for his brilliant rhetorical accomplishments): 'We make out of the quarrel with others, rhetoric, but of the quarrel with ourselves, poetry'. I think of Hopkins' struggle with his mind and mood and how the urgency and uniqueness of his work was born from this.

Do we want arguments in poetry? Richard Dixon's critique of Hopkins, which I would reclaim as praise, comes to mind: poetry should be like chunks of 'impracticable quartz'. An argument is an attempt to influence others, but poetic influence is not won through changing people's mind about a fixed view but through crystallising complex emotions into language that allows us to make our own sense. Viewpoints are already too simplified. Poets putting across arguments that everyone else knows is a windy business. 'We hate', John Keats wrote in a letter, years before any of these Norwood poets put pen-to-paper, 'poetry that has a palpable design upon us'.

Yarrow's poetry, I tell Colin now, is overly rhetorical. He had energy and was productive and I've captured that in the phrase I place down at his grave here: STARTLED AIR. Yet his work is defined — or not defined — by a kind of startling airiness. Little is known of his life: we have only the work to go on. The most I could find is this mention in Catherine Reilly's *Mid-Victorian Poetry, 1860-1879*:

> YARROW, JOHN (1817-98). Orator, painter, and professor of elocution. Lived at 24 Trigon Terrace, Clapham Road, London SW. Died at 31 Howard Road, Cricklewood, Middlesex.

As with Blanchard there is confusion over his date of birth: is the date in the book wrong, or is it the tombstone, which has been permanently debossed with 1818? His life and work are hazy and the digital book market does little to aid this. Whereas Lowry's work has been scanned, OCRd, given a free platform online and is available to buy and 'Look Inside' by Amazon, Yarrow's books remain cloistered in the cloth of their original print. I do find his *Shakespeare: a Tercentenery* online at readanypoem.com. The text has been dumped, unproofed and masticated through a digital image of a Kindle screen — the software aspiring towards hardware. The text itself is flawed with errors, the formatting of the heavy iambic stresses fallen into a dated slagheap — a clodded mound — of prose. It is the greatest insult to any dead poet to have their work not just unread, but butchered.

Yet his work invites decimation. Finding a copy of *Shakespeare* later I am aghast at its superficial advocacy of all that is unquestionably great in 'The Bard' and Yarrow's writing is the poetic equivalent of bath-time back-scratching:

> Language is mute; my bosom throbs with fear
> While contemplating the conception grand
> That hath for centuries amaz'd our land and
> Nor ours alone. The list'ning earth accords
> Spontaneous admiration : some stand
> Stricken with wonder and some murmur solemn words,
> Or, breathe, in awe. His name, whose mind such wealth
>   affords!

Heavy with the tropes of an antiquated rhetoric, it is difficult to read through as much as five or six lines at a time. The placing of the adjective after the noun — 'conception grand', 'centuries amaz'd' — is instantly wearing. This is poetry written as if Romanticism had never happened, harking — and harking is the verb here — back to the worst of the Augustans.[22]

A twig breaks behind me: Colin is clearing up some roughage. It's time for us to leave. I accidentally kick a stone across the path in front of me. A stone that has no words on it. I pick it up: spoors of black moss have spread themselves across its surface, petrifying it with an umbra of living shade. The cold permanence of stone is a myth.

Stone is a breeding ground for new life.

In the Catacombs

In those sad words I took farewell:
Like echoes in sepulchral halls,
As drop by drop the water falls
In vaults and catacombs, they fell;

And, falling, idly broke the peace
Of hearts that beat from day to day,
Half-conscious of their dying clay,
And those cold crypts where they shall cease.

The high Muse answer'd: "Wherefore grieve
Thy brethren with a fruitless tear?
Abide a little longer here,
And thou shalt take a nobler leave."

Alfred Lord Tennyson, *In Memoriam*

WE'RE SITTING IN A CAFÉ on Norwood High Street, overlooking the cemetery gates, a month after the opening of *Curious*. It's another of those perfect summer days when the world seems to slow down, the car wheels whispering *here comes the night*, though the night never seems to come. We've been talking about how my writing is going, then Colin, changing track, makes me an offer into the underworld: would I like to go down into the catacombs?

I've always liked the word, its anapaestic rush of early syllables outriding inexorably towards the leisurely final syllable. Cat-a-comb; from the Late Latin *catacumba: among the tombs*. I don't say Yes, I don't have to; we're already walking like delinquents up Norwood High Street. I walk into the road and step back in time for a truck to pass. I take a breath, glutting on the little air the heatwave gives. The important thing about heading into the underworld is of course not to look back, but I need to remember to look ahead too.

The thing about Colin is that — yes, I remember now — he's a management consultant by trade. He brings the same professionalism to his pastime of taking care of the cemetery. I'm a keen amateur and need to remember to follow his lead. He's done this before. His dead are not actors or puppets, their lives as real as ours is to us now, sitting in his green Skoda — the low-fuel light flashing — ready to drive towards the centre of the cemetery. This is why he takes my search for a poet so seriously: the work the living do for the dead is the only hope they have.

We could have walked but today is all about speed. Catch the summer before it goes. The scaffold around the dilapidated chapel above the catacombs comes into view. A fox looks back at us as we leave the car — it's leaner and a deeper red than its inner-city relatives.

Colin leads me to a set of steps leading down into the catacombs. There's a scaffold above, holding together the joins of the new building against what's left of the bombed chapel. Colin lifts a blue net and we leave the sun behind; the coolness of Victorian brick and moss rises from below ground-level.

We pass a ceramic tube of Doulton's pipe, the architectural equivalent of Tennyson's octosyllabic lines. A vessel for so much shit to flow through. Colin hands me one of two thick black torches, reminiscent of a deep sea diver's lights. The thick iron doors of the catacombs resist at first and then clang out our freedom: the day disappears behind us.

The underworld is always beneath us — this is something that every poet knows. We walk above our own resting places for the time that we have left. A moment from Dickens' *Dombey and Son* comes to mind — written a decade after West Norwood was opened — when the cold, ambitious Dombey takes his son Paul (the name of my father and — through the variant Pavel — of my son) to be christened. 'Over the fireplace was a ground-plan of the vaults underneath the church'. There is something reassuring about the paid-for order of the vaults beneath when one is alive and well above ground. We take up new rituals. We go on.

There is a box of red switches on the wall as we enter and Colin presses them down. A distant light goes on across the emptiness. What look like black telephone booths are evenly arranged across the walls: small rooms set-back from the vast hall we're inside. Directly in front of us is a machine that might have been used as a device for torture. It exists in the hinge between ritualistic and industrial practices. A compression device for witches. A shrinking tool for growing chimney sweeps.

"This," says Colin, "is the catafalque. It's basically a coffin lift". He points up to the roof and there's a hole the same size as the iron bed that's attached to the machine. "After the service there would be a vicar's assistant standing there" and he points to a dark corner of the passage. He tells me that the vicar would have given the nod to the man controlling the hydraulic action pump (who must have been in good shape: it took 180 pumps of the handle to raise the bed to its full height). Amazingly for its time the machine was operated by hydraulics and operated silently. As the body descended from view the vicar might read from Jude: *Unto him that is able to keep us from falling*. The family wouldn't have to wait long to reunite — a family vault was bought forever. I think of them as the equivalent to the middle-class obsession for Range Rovers: a comfortable space for the whole family to travel from life towards the promise of eternity.[23]

The catafalque, or coffin lift, described by Peter Ackroyd as 'part antiquity and part theatre.' (Photograph: Nick Catford.)

I have no reason to suspect there's another poet and it strikes me now that there's no purpose to me being down here other than to be amongst the dead. I've become death obsessed. I'll follow any road to the underworld. No hints have appeared through my research, no suggestions in the books of the notable dead. I think of the 12 dead poets above me in the ground. Their skulls form node-points in the network of metrical language.

I stumble forward with the torch. The place is a labyrinth: corridors lead from corridors. It reminds me of how architecture in the stories of Edgar Allen Poe is always symbolic of the mind, an idea later picked up in the horror films of Dario Argento, where cupboards lead to rooms of barbed wire and then out, inexplicably, into the forecourts of inner-city cathedrals. Not knowing what is around the corner it is very tempting for the mind to fill in the gaps. Later, I'll research the layout of the catacombs and find them mathematically designed in regimented honeycombs. When I see the map, it strikes me as a pattern poem shaped like George Herbert's 'Easter Wings'. An exoskeleton of a moth. Or perhaps a structural

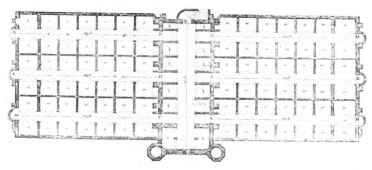

Structural map of the catacombs at West Norwood Cemetery.

device for a poem, like Swinburne's roundel.[24] I'm starting to see death as poetry-shaped.

We're still inside the main thoroughfare of the catacomb, the thorax of the moth's body from where the forewings and hindwings extend way beyond what seems possible from such a slim column. Like a moth too, there are two eyes at the base of the main corridor: a structure than seems made for flight but is constructed for immortal stasis.

We turn into another corridor. Like the floors of a hotel booked by the families of a marriage party, whole clusters of vaults have been taken up with the same surnames: the Webbs and Butts in Bay 9, the Frooms and Wellingtons in Bay 10, the Poppletons and Wrights in Bay 7.

Stacked bays of individual coffins in the catacombs.
(Photograph: Nick Catford.)

There are also loose coffins stacked on the open shelving of the public vaults. The coffins are air-stacked like half-bricks though they give the impression of floating. They appear strangely in transit as if the process of their burial was abandoned. The wood of the coffins surrounding their lead-lined interior has splayed and warped through the decades of fluctuating humidity. I remember when my dad died that we had to make a decision about how much money to spend on the wood of the coffin, which was essentially to be lowered into the earth and decimated by the ecosystem of insect life.[25] With this kind of burial the finish of the wood is everything: voyeurs arrive here over one 150 years later, shining torches and making judgements. There is good reason to spend time selecting the right grain and varnish.

Colin points underneath the shelves of public burials and tells me of the graveyard attendant who was arrested years before for hiding over three million pounds of cocaine in the dank, hidden corner he's pointing at. The dust of life and the dust of death. The ego, they say, rides on the rush of amphetamines. There is good competition for paranoia too, amidst the grandeur of heavyweight Victorians.

To Colin's surprise, after years of trawling the catacombs alone, there is a moth resident on a family plate. In the airless vacuum it has fluttered, settled and transisted into death.

Looking through the loculi of the vaults is a disconcerting form of voyeurism: here are the dead that paid to be looked at. Time has been kinder to the tinder of some coffins more than others. Although by law every coffin in a catacomb had to be lined with lead there are cases in which the wood has buckled and collapsed around its inner frame. There are also instances where even the lead has fractured at its joints, enough to show the greying splints of human bone.

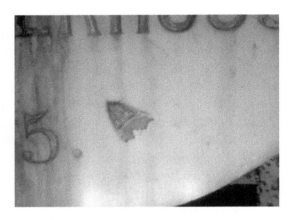

Aside from some of the unidentifiable remains I've found in the Thames, this is my first experience of looking at human bone. The bones I can see have been cremated but not put through a cremulator: burnt but not pulverised. The bone has a friable white delicateness, shards that could be snapped like Sunday dinner wishbones.

"If you touch any live flesh", Colin says, "there's a chance of catching smallpox or anthrax." I look closely between a crumbled coffin lid and its lead-lined interior and see tiny pieces of text, from a Victorian newspaper, packed between the layers. I see one word in a miniscule font: 'madam'.

Colin asks me to speak two words to hear back the echo and without thinking I summon the name of a 19th century figure and hear his name recede: "Charles Lyle, *Charles Lyle*, *Charles Lyle*..." One of my poets was a Miller and, in the dark, I spot another: his nameplate beautifully illustrated in red-on-black lettering like a concrete poem of the 1950s. The dying battery on the torch strains to find the M on the Miller (no relation to the basket-weaving poet that Dickens rejected).

Colin points out a writer's connection: high above us on the top-shelf of a vault is Edith Nesbit's father and sister. The coffin of her sister Mary is peculiarly shaped and has what looks like a relockable keyhole with iron clasps and a fleur-de-lis. Colin tells me how she was sent to the French Pyrenees after contracting TB but it was too late: she died at 18 and was shipped back in the coffin of another climate.

I take my phone from my pocket and find that there are three white bars displayed, indicating a network. 3G for the RIP community. As Colin dusts off the rusted flakes off a vault window I check Nesbit's Wikipedia page. Between 1886 and 1922 she wrote 22 poetry books, including the wonderfully titled *Jesus in London*. It is never difficult to find evidence to bear out my theory that there's a poet in every family, though Edith Nesbit isn't buried here: the poetic connection is through association only.[26]

There's something rattling in my pocket, stone-like circles attached to elastic. I take it out: it's a half-finished confectionary necklace that I had promised to give to my son, Pavel, when we were walking to school a few mornings ago but which we'd both forgotten about. The once-urgent emotions of all the families down here suddenly seems very real: death is something that goes wrong to excited children, all the plans and promises of families are made null over time. I remind myself that words remain. Art remains. Life stories remain. This feeling isn't quite one of panic, though the vision of the eternity of time after our lives is extremely disconcerting. All of us know this, though sometimes the fact seems realer than at other times — poets often stare at this darkness for so long they lose their daytime vision. Being surrounded by the ordinary dead who also once shared sweets on a school morning in summer is a dark epiphany down here, where there is no spangle from the sun, no dance of Autumn leaves. I put the ring of sweets back in my pocket for when Pavel wakes up on Saturday morning and Dadda's back from London.

In the dark, the white chalk scratching underfoot, my torch flashes on a name and I stop in amusement: John Bonus. He must have lived on a gameshow host's diet as his coffin, stacked on a lower shelf of the loculus, is monumental. His name-plate is resplendent in azure blue. Colin gives me the area code as Bay 1, vault E, though I have no sense of how this relates to where I am standing.

Later that evening, when I'm back above ground and writing up my account of visiting the catacombs, I find that John Bonus's daughter was Anna Kingsford (1846-1888), the first woman in the UK to achieve a medical degree. She was a campaigner for women's rights, an anti-vivisectionist and a seer of other spiritual dimensions. She was also a poet. Discovering her father by chance, drawn to his name on an unplanned journey into the catacombs, begins to spiral my research in another direction. She called her visionary prose pieces 'Illuminations', a connection to Rimbaud's book of the same title written just years before in both London and Paris — the same cities as Kingsford lived in — which offers a direction along further Victorian corridors and coincidences that I have to follow.

This is where I leave myself, with Colin, standing in the catacombs and ask you to walk back up the Anglican stairs and into the barely brighter streets of London in the 1870s. The absence of Anna Kingsford's coffin in the family vault opens up a window that we can see through — past the name of John Bonus — into a life that went on to achieve so much against the winds of Victorian male society. Could it be that Kingsford's achievement as a poet might be beyond Smedley's? I follow the links too quick to realise that I'm breaking the boundaries I've set myself and by the time I realise I'm too deep within her story to withdraw; the appearance of her father, John Bonus, at a séance, and her connection with one of the greatest poets of the 19th century, Arthur Rimbaud have taken hold of me. At this point of realisation, her story has already written itself into mine.

Anna Kingsford.

Kingsford's visions were published later under the title *Clothed with the Sun*. The similarity with my own *Clotted Sun* — a title borrowed from Capetanakis — turns the random encounter into something both strange and imminent because connected through language. *Clothed. Clotted.* The triangle of myself, Kingsford and Capetanakis forms through the strength of a syllable.

I think of the red fox I passed as we left Colin's Skoda — the knowing, backwards-look it had given us. Anna Kingsford later become one of the most vociferous anti-vivisectionists of the period, claiming that she only undertook a medical degree to work towards alleviating the suffering caused by animal testing.[27] When she was younger Anna had enjoyed taking part in fox-hunting until after one hunt she was seized with a vision of seeing the world from the fox's perspective. I have never been a spiritualist — though have documented three months of trying to talk to God through the poetry of Hopkins and Herbert in my sequence *Sudden Trellises* — but have always been a keen maker and pursuer of connections: the fox in the sun, watching Colin and I dig downwards, provides a rich poetic

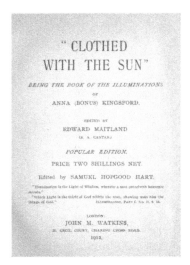

Clothed with the Sun, Kingsford's
posthumous book of 'Illuminations'.

connection. A Thought Fox. A journey towards dead poets should be rich with metaphors and stress patterns; they are the DNA of poetic investigation.

Anna Kingsford was born in 1846 in Stratford, Essex. This was where my poet-without-equal, G.M. Hopkins, had been born two years before. Kingsford began to write poetry from a young age, an activity that was very closely connected with the development of her spiritual life.

My research takes me later into the night, the dust of the catacombs still fresh on my shoulders. I have a stack of books I picked up from the library after leaving the cemetery. I open the laptop and light up the internet. There is a moth circling the keyboard, clinking its ceramic wings against the glass of the screen.

I discover that John Bonus spoke to his daughter four years after his death. This is from Kingsford's perspective and the viewpoint of all genuine spiritualists never wavers with equivocation. She had started to take séances at the house of a medium called Miss Theobald. A message came through addressed to Miss Bonus: "My child, resist the materialistic teachings you have learned. There is a future, for I — your father — *live*. Seek earnestly … Avoid underdevelopment by prayer to God. No other form". Miss Theobald later wrote to Kingsford's collaborator and editor Edward Maitland: 'presently a message came purporting to be from her father. He said how sorry he was to have brought her up in such erroneous ideas, and urged her to investigate spiritualism, as it would bring evidence of the future state, and of his power to come to her and help her.'

Kingsford heard what she wanted to hear and she resisted materialism all her life. She sent her poems to Maitland, saying that they were written 'before I was seventeen, and many when I was a child of ten or eleven'. I read her poems. My conclusion comes quick: Kingsford could write good verse by the standards of the time, though she never attempted to push form — or develop a style — with the same uniqueness as she applied to her other passions. Maitland is no close-reader of poetry though he is quick to spot the 'unconscious imitations of various styles, especially that of the 'In Memoriam''. The best poem in the volume is the title piece in which Kingsford uses subtly changing stress patterns to create a lyrical music that is much more impressive than the metallic clank of her Norwood peers à Beckett and Talfourd:

> Reeds in the river! Reeds in the river!
> O deep in my heart like the reeds in the river,
> My thoughts grow in darkness, far down out of sight,
> And over my life passes shadow and light,
> Like sunshine and cloud on the breast of the stream;
> But I sit by the banks of my river and dream,
> For day after day they grow silent and strong,
> The reeds of my Syrinx, the reeds of my song.

The end-rhymes may be obvious and somewhat trite here, but the verse is compact and flows without awkwardness. What is fascinating about this poem is the split of the poet's own self; how her heart and her thoughts can be beneath the river and by the side of the river at the same time. The poetry provides a way in to Kingsford's life and mind — her manic phases within various creative forms and her ability to assume voices and hear the minds of dead people.[28] If she were alive today she might have been given treatment for schizophrenia.[29] In Kingsford's poem her multiple selves manifest in the imagery of submerged and bankside dissolution. Her body and mind are both dead and live: she is voyeur and observed at the same time. The reeds themselves provide a useful metaphor for wrestling with these ideas: they are a part of the river and are both beneath and above at the same time.

It is as if Kingsford lost interest in poetry as her concerns became more fiercely attached to her social concerns (the struggle for women's liberations and the rights of animals) and the spiritual life beyond. Poetry had been a way of joining up both places, though she had never used poetry for political purposes and as her gifts as a seer became stronger it is easy to see that any concerns with prosody would have been a distraction from the vision in front of her (hence the move into prose). Not all of the poems she wrote were as successful as the one quoted above; much of her language is archaic and her metrical and rhyming structures often clunky. One poem ('Salem's Sea') begins with the unforgettable disjunction: 'Prick fast, fair knight; the west is gray'.

Her collection *River Reeds* was reviewed in *The Athenaeum* in 1875 and the reviewer offers a very generous view of her limited gifts as a poet, though in a way that is patronising and revealing of his views on what great poetry should be: 'The author has a pretty knack of versification; her lines are polished, her language is well chosen, and she has some power of thought ... It is refreshing to be able to notice for once a new book of poems without having to enter our usual protest against bad rhyme, slipshod metre, and ungrammatical English'.[30] The reviewer is right that there is certainly 'versification' here and — as with all her undertakings — power of thought. The reviewer is mistaken in attempting to measure poetry by grammatical English (it was this kind of narrow view of poetry that would give Cummings, Pound and Hopkins such a tide to push against). Kingsford was a good poet in her age though there is none of the radical edge and innovation which I have been looking for in my dead.

Thinking of the cold plate of Portland stone I was looking at a few hours ago, clinically cut with the text FAMILY CATACOMB OF JOHN BONUS, doesn't prepare me for the dedication in *River Reeds*:

> To you, our Father in Paradise, whom living, we did
> clearly love, your little daughter dedicates.

Grief, captured in language, has a way of transcending even the death of the person who felt it.

John Bonus was a successful ship owner and his death gave his daughter financial stability with an annual income of £700 a

Torchlight on the family catacomb of John Bonus.

year. He had stipulated that this money could not be shared with a husband, which no doubt filled Kingsford with the conviction to be able to discuss terms of freedom before she married her cousin

Algernon Kingsford in 1867. Algernon was an Anglican Priest whose constituency was in Atcham: the burial place, I see, for Kingsford. The gap in the family vault here is answered through her marriage. Remarkably for a woman of this time, when Kingsford married Algernon she made clear beforehand that she would not sacrifice any of her aspirations and the freedom she would need to fulfil them. Algernon was happy to accept her terms.

In 1873 Kingsford met Edward Maitland, and they entered into a curiously binding collaborative relationship which they maintained was platonic but did invite public speculation. Maitland arrived at the right moment as Kingsford wanted to begin her medical degree in Paris but due to the conventions of the time couldn't travel or live alone in a foreign city. Algernon persuaded Maitland to travel with her as he himself couldn't leave his constituency. Maitland had been widowed for 20 years and was instantly drawn to Kingsford's mind, work and, as he described it himself, beauty. He immediately accepted. Maitland would co-write the lectures that went to make up the book *The Perfect Way* (published in 1881), and after Kingsford's death would also write her biography and edit and oversee the publishing of *Clothed with the Sun*.

As Alan Pert has pointed out in the only subsequent biography of Kingsford since Maitland's, *Red Cactus*, Maitland's accounts and views of Kingsford should be questioned. He was not free of the conventions of the time and had his own agenda which Anna helped to fulfil. He was a large man with a high domed head and as Florence Fenwick Miller recorded in her autobiography at this time, he was: 'old (55 or so), plain, heavy, and dull of conversation'. He had the innocuous look of a soon-to-be-retired postman who suffers from the megalomania of Phileas Fogg. As Pert has pointed out, although he clearly revered Kingsford and helped her to pursue many of her causes, there was something of the Dr Frankenstein about him, keeping daily journal records on her eccentricities, views and movements.

Maitland wrote that Kingsford was 'entrusted to my charge expressly in order that by my study of her I might recover for the

Edward Maitland. (*The Life of Anna Kingsford*, 1893.)

world's benefit the long-lost knowledge of the soul's being, nature and history'. It is when Maitland questions Kingsford's marriage to Algernon Kingsford — 'a marriage in little more than name' — we might suspect his feelings for Kingsford to be beyond mere companionship and the sharing of interests. The inference here is that he was her real husband (and Kingsford was dead at this point, lying in the ground of her husband's manor). There is no respect for how radical Algernon was at this time in deciding to marry on Kingsford's terms, which were — as she put it in a letter — 'to be independent and free'. Kingsford was walking against the wind of Victorian conventions with a mime-rope: 'I only wonder that he took me,' she wrote.

Algernon was Kingsford's cousin and an Anglican Priest. There was to be a further twist of the fleur-de-lis in his ribs as soon after their marriage she converted to Roman Catholicism. They had a daughter together called Eadith, though Kingsford soon became disillusioned as a mother when the relationship didn't develop as planned. Like poetry, Eadith became a concern that distanced as Kingsford's careering spiritual life intensified. Kingsford had the ambition and single-mindedness of a genius, though she was splitting the outcomes between the spiritual and scientific: she needed the playroom of her mind to be free for her own pursuits.

Maitland accompanied her to Paris and they frequented London together on her return. They spent most of their time together and wrote intense letters recounting incidents with the spirits when they were apart. Like many people who spend a lot of time together, they had fallings-out; Maitland maintained that this was due to dark spirits trying to come between them. In January 1877 Kingsford had written to Maitland from her room in Chelsea: 'I cannot do real, worthy, and valuable work apart from you. I think your magnetism imparts a vigour to my brain which nothing else gives me…You *must* be one with me'. She went on to write that she had felt compelled — in a state of trance-lucidity after looking at the moon — to write to Maitland. Maitland then wrote back to say that he had been visited that morning by his dead ex-wife, who said she had been with someone called 'Mary', which — as they both knew — was Anna's spiritual name. Maitland, in an unembarrassed moment of potential husbandry, tells her that he had noticed her face closely resembling his ex-wife that morning. It is easy to read the distillation of their attraction as so far repressed and pushed beneath the cortex of the impossible that it begins to appear as spirits on a plane beyond the physical. Their relationship was not straightforward.

Kingsford wrote this poem for Maitland in December 1875:

> Here, by the sea, which must part us, I stand,
>   Looking the last of my love in your face,
> Feeling the touch of your hand on my hand,
>   Only, alas! For so little space;
> Hope on my lips, dear, but fear in my heart,
> Lest not for a time but for ever we part.

This is verse of straightforward love and longing. The strong emotion she had for him is obvious. She was married and they never would be: all of their longings are trapped inside the spirits that visit them.

At the point of writing this poem Rimbaud had left poetry behind forever. His poetry was far more original and futuristic than anything Kingsford — or any occasional reader of poetry — could have conceived as possible at this time. When Kingsford wrote her first poem in 1855, when she was just nine, Rimbaud had only just been born. Thirteen years later he wrote his first poem and, shortly after that, his own *Illuminations*. These two radical minds are bound by their work of the same name, which were both attempts to do justice to the belief they had in their ability as seers.

It has been a long day, the kind that seems to stretch forever and might be best ended by falling to sleep on a massive lawn looking up at the stars. Yet I'm looking through to a different world, following links from Anna Kingsford's life into Arthur Rimbaud's. I feel something in my pocket: it is the ring of sweets for Pavel. I bite one off the elastic: midnight sugar-rush. The connections keep taking place and I follow them willingly into the early hours of the next morning, wanting to know if these two outsiders, who had both defined themselves as seers, had physically crossed the same streets, had been in the same room, had even so much as glanced at each other.[31]

They were both living between Paris and London from 1873 onwards. There is no chance that Kingsford would have known Rimbaud by name; the avant-garde poet who would remain unpublished until 1886. At this point Kingsford was back and living in England after catching the pneumonia that would lead to her death. Rimbaud read voraciously and without parameters, across literature, science, political and spiritual literature. He may have come across *River Reeds* (unlikely) or her spiritual work with Maitland, *The Key of the Creeds*, published in 1875 (more likely). Unfortunately there are no records of what items Rimbaud called up at the readings rooms of the British Museum. The hours of skulking through the fog of Bloomsbury are as obscure as his last years under the sun of Aden, Yemen, where he'd gone in search of a new identity — or at least the shaking-off of the old one.

Their paths form a curious cross-trail of flight to — and exit from — London and Paris between the years 1871 and 1875. Rimbaud had arrived in Paris first, from Charleville, to meet the poet Verlaine in September 1871. Rimbaud had written him two letters, the second enclosing a poem, to which Verlaine had written back: 'Come, dear great soul. We await you; we desire you', sending him a one-way ticket to Paris. From the moment of their meeting the younger poet had an instant hold over Verlaine (whose wife had just given birth). Within weeks Verlaine was having to explain the scars on his legs (from Rimbaud stabbing him) and questioning why his beer was frothing peculiarly (Rimbaud had added sulphuric acid when he wasn't looking). They ran away together, arriving in London in September 1872, and after a dutiful return home to France for Christmas they were both back in January.

Rimbaud grew increasingly frustrated with Verlaine and everything that society had to offer, capturing this frustration in *A Season in Hell* - written between April and August 1873.

It was in that August that Kingsford and Maitland began to correspond and she had sent him her poems with a note to say: 'read them with mercy' (it could be said that the opposite is true of *A Season in Hell*: that the author had no concern for showing mercy to his reader). Both Kingsford and Rimbaud — if in completely different places with their poetic gifts — shared a similar disgust for the world around them. Kingsford wrote to Maitland: 'love I fail to see ... I see everywhere prevailing the Rule of the Strong ... I see everywhere slaughter, suffering, and terror'. There is a similarity of tone and disgust in *A Season in Hell* when Rimbaud rails: 'I have never belonged to this race ... I do not understand your laws' ('Bad Blood'). By November 1873, four months after Rimbaud and Verlaine's relationship had climaxed with Rimbaud shooting Verlaine in the wrist in a hotel room in Brussels, Rimbaud was back in Paris, working as a waiter and then, according to Graham Robb, selling keyrings and bootlaces on the streets.

Just months after Rimbaud and Verlaine had trashed the room of their relationship, Kingsford and Maitland physically met for the first time in London: the attraction was as instant. Maitland wrote: 'Never had I seen anyone so completely and intensely alive, or comprising so many diverse and incompatible personalities'. Kingsford was having strong visions at this point (she had shown Maitland the account she'd written of The Fall which had come to her in a dream) and although not yet calling them 'Illuminations' Maitland would give her the confidence and encouragement to begin to write these down for posterity.[32]

Maitland said that both he and Kingsford had believed themselves to be living in 'Bible times' and her 'Illuminations' are, as she says in No. IV, 'reveilations, or reveilings …There can be no true or worthy illumination which destroys distances and exposes the details of things'. Kingsford offers visions which draw heavily on well-known stories, or scenarios, which then become platforms for moral instruction:

1. You ask the method and nature of Inspiration, and the means whereby God reveleath Truth.
2. Know that there is no enlightenment from without: the secret of things is revealed from within.
3. From without cometh no Divine Revelation: but the Spirit within beareth witness.
4. Think not I tell you that which you know not: for except you know it, it cannot be given to you.

In contrast Rimbaud's *Illuminations* are not a place to go to for ethical advice: 'My wisdom is as neglected as chaos is' ('Lives I'). Rimbaud offers no visions from the next life to show us how to live in this one. Rimbaud's role — or anti-role — as a 'voyant' is to show us the complete degradation of humanity: 'Behold the age of Murderers' ('Morning of Drunkeness'). His *Illuminations* are split into five sections, 'Childhood', 'Life of the Poet', 'Nature', 'City' and — interesting for comparison to Kingsford's work — 'Mystic Vision'. Rimbaud simply presents his visions of Biblical activity as something that is happening at the same time as numerous other kinds of movement and activity. The poems move with cinematic speed from one image to the next, with no time to weigh up any moral significance:

> On the slope of the hill, the angels whirl their woollen
> robes in the steel and emerald grasses.
> Meadows of flame leap up to the top of the rise.

This was written in the year Maitland had met Kingsford and she had announced the visionary dreams which would later become her 'Illuminations'. There is a strong parallel between the images occupying the minds of the two voyants at this precise moment in history. As with Rimbaud's poem above, Kingsford captures angels rising upwards to the skies:

> A golden chalice, like those used in Catholic rites, but
> having three linings, was given to me in my sleep by
> an Angel. These linings, he told me, signified the three
> degrees of the heavens — purity of life, purity of heart,
> and purity of doctrine.

Both Rimbaud and Kingsford, with their different concerns and literary ambitions, pushed their bodies through rational boundaries to achieve prescience in their life. Although Kingsford would not do this poetically, her spiritual writings have had a huge legacy over later spiritualists, including Gandhi. Her formal poetry did not push the conventions of the time and has been forgotten with good reason, yet her spiritual thinking had a great impact on W.B. Yeats, who featured her briefly in his unfinished novel *The Speckled Bird*.

Humphrey Hare in his *Portrait for a Sketch of Rimbaud* captures Rimbaud's anti-spiritualism succinctly when he writes: 'Rimbaud's was not a renunciation of the spiritual, but a spiritual renunciation'. His *Illuminations* were the opposite of Kingsford's: they were a way of *giving up* on the possibility of finding a 'truth' and not the beginnings of a quest to find it.

This is the period when Rimbaud and Kingsford would have been most likely to pass each other; from March 1874 Rimbaud was living on Stamford Street, adjacent to Waterloo Station. Maitland would go to Paris with Kingsford in April to enrol for her medical degree, which would begin in the Autumn. Kingsford stayed in London throughout this summer and although we don't know her address we do know that Maitland lived at Thurloe Square, South Kensington. Maitland wrote about them talking together in a 'picture gallery' which is very likely to be the V&A. In June Rimbaud moved from Stamford Street to a road close to his original Howland Street address he'd shared with Verlaine. His mother and sister arrived to stay with him in July and he took them on a tour of the sights: his metropolitan student days had graduated into the careering plight of the experienced Londoner. According to his sister, Rimbaud was armed with statistical information on everything — his radical attack against organised knowledge was so readily normalised for his family.

Rimbaud didn't return home to France until later in December, at which point Kingsford was back in London, enrolled in a course in physiology at a school for women in Henrietta Street and pursuing further studies in medicine and botany at the Regent's Park School (this would have formed part of her medical degree). This is where I see their paths crossing, along the Northern Line route that connects Leicester Square to Tottenham Court Road and Goodge Street. Anna's studies in Henrietta Street were only a mile from Rimbaud's Howland Street.[33] With their heads full of illuminated visions of the physical city and the spiritual and anti-spiritual plight of its inhabitants, the bodies of the two poets passed each other through the unlit streets of London.

Anna Kingsford was buried in Atcham, with all that an above-ground funeral has to offer. The earth's loaminess accepts the body in a more complete and finished way than the public archive system of the catacombs. A local newspaper described the burial: 'The coffin was lowered into its last resting place — an ordinary grave — in the midst of a heavy snowstorm, and in the presence of perhaps not more than a score of spectators'.

Kingsford and Rimbaud have parted but Rimbaud now wants me to himself. I know it's late but I stay with him for a while — perhaps I need the endorphin rush of incredible poetry to end the day. Rimbaud was a poet comfortable with the catacombs: he saw the whole transparent palaces of the future cities as built upon them. He could see the decay beneath the grandeur. I flick through the *Illuminations* — images of tombs and coffins dominate:

> The chateau's up for sale and the shutters are coming loose. — The priest must have taken away the key of the church ('Childhood — II')
>
> Now hire for me the tomb, whitewashed with the lines of cement in bold relief — far underground ('Childhood

— V')

Death whistles and rings of muffled music cause this
worshipped body to rise up, expand, and tremble like a
ghost. Scarlet and black wounds break out on the proud
flesh...Our bones are reclothed with a new and amorous
body ('Being Beauteous')

I have invigorated my blood. I am released from my
duty. I must not think of that any longer. I am really from
beyond the tomb and without work. ('Lives — III')

Coffins, too, under their dark canopy with their pitch-
black plumes ('Ruts')

The modern city to Rimbaud was just another manifestation of
modern thought and like all manifestations of modern thought was
built upon the lines laid down by the dead. Victorian glass domes
are built upon blackening tombs. For him death was always the
unequivocal end; yet the afterlife of his work has endured without
equal amongst his contemporaries. Rimbaud has become our first
truly modern poet, the one most cited amongst young poets and
musicians railing against their own sense of the unjust rationality
and ill-reasoning of the corporate world.

'I am released from my duty,' he writes — yet I want to hold
on to Rimbaud for just a little while longer. The journey with Anna
Kingsford has offered an unforeseen diversion to the day. After the
unclear journey through the dark of the catacombs I find myself
emerging on the other side to walk with her through the 1870s. Yet
she is not the poet I'm looking for and I need to make these pauses in
my journey — late at night, early morning, whenever — to be fed by

the poets who remind me what can be achieved in the art.

For Rimbaud the capacity to be able to *see beyond* the limits of the society he lived in was very much bound with creating a new poetic language that would allow the truth to be seen. As he writes in a to his teacher Georges Izambard in a letter of 13 May 1871:

> Now, I am degrading myself as much as possible. Why? I want to be a poet, and I am working to make myself a seer: you will not understand this, and I don't know how to explain it to you. It is a question of reaching the unknown by the derangement of all the senses. The sufferings are enormous, but one had to be strong, one had to be born a poet, and I know I am a poet. This is not at all my fault.

For the poet the political is always personal. Rimbaud allowed the crises of his time — in morality, materialism, spiritualism — to be played out through his mind and body. To do this he had to find

Arthur Rimbaud. (Photograph: Unknown.)

a new poetic form: the condensed prose poem. This was a form that allowed him to knit together different languages and modes of thinking into a coherent if incredibly dense whole. *Illuminations* is something of a compendium of poetic innovation; Rimbaud could have given a new form to each of the 12 Norwood poets and still had some left over. *Illuminations* contains two of the first free verse poems written in French, 'Marine' and 'Movement'. The relationship between thinking outside social constraints and language is contiguous; Rimbaud asserts that to be able to say what was previously unsayable requires a radical approach to poetic form. His mind, as Hughes says of Dickinson, is 'the crucible' in which social upheaval is recorded in poetry. His metrics encase the meltdown of the previous order.

The 42 poems in the *Illuminations* show Rimbaud continually reinventing the kind of poetry he needs to allow him to express this crisis most effectively. The reader enters a mesmeric spectropia of language: especially when reading late at night.[34] We oscillate between the macro- and micro-cosmic, ride the jump-cuts within shifting panoramas, detach and reattach ourselves to subjective and objective voices, assimilate classical references alongside the ultra-modern, follow linear stories that terminate in the condensed lyric, unpick meta-poetic references until poetic language is left hollowed of meaning ('The boredom of saying 'dear body', 'dear heart'.'), balance narrative and metonymic dual-meanings, witness the invention of a prose sonnet, delight in the 'musical phrase', handle found texts, and are continually pulled in and pushed away through the introduction of genre after genre, the dramatic monologue, imagistic reduction ('the wild crowd wanders under the bare trees'), confession ('In a wine cellar I learned history'), love poetry and allegory. This lexicon of possibilities is casually and aggressively laid before us with a Punk self-assurance: Rimbaud shows he *could* write in straightforward formal verse but what does straightforward verse have to do with the urgent times he was living through?

Jeremy Reed, in his poem on Rimbaud, pictures the French poet as *still* running, away from the materialistic struggle for order and knowledge of the 1870s, towards the Horn of Africa, where he arrived in 1880 at the hinge of a new decade. Humphrey Hare imagines him at this point in his life unaware that 'eleven years of life... remained — years filled with boredom, pain and disappointment — his efforts were to be directed towards gaining a competence, the price of freedom'. Rimbaud would never return to poetry although his travels were recorded in most geographical publications of the time. Once he was settled in Africa he seems to have spent his efforts learning technical skills and working in the coffee trade (with a sideline in weapons). Rimbaud the Punk, the runaway libertine, died in 1891 (three years after Anna) and was buried at home, in Charleville, his last days tended by the sister whom he had guided through London with such flair.

There is a memorable image of Rimbaud, hobbling on the one leg remaining after cancer had led to the removal of the other, convincing himself and his sister that everything would be okay if he could just get back to Africa. They got as far as Paris before — exhausted and in cold sweats — they were forced to turn back to Charleville. The poet who had stormed away from his home town to reinvent poetry in London and Paris, returned home to his bedroom to die. His sister said that he took confession before he died, though his myth — like the speculation around Emily Dickinson's love affairs — was very probably invented by his sister to create the image of her brother that she wanted. *Her* Rimbaud is not the one that has obsessed readers — and poets — for well over a century. We are yet to arrive at a point of full understanding of his work.

Blake was right: all moments of history take place at the same time. When I walked down that dark corridor of the catacombs I also made an unexpected turn in my narrative. It is too late to read more. It is unclear how Rimbaud even arrived here. The catacombs of today are still so vivid. I walk back through the vault to the other side, where I left Colin and myself a little while earlier. I shine the torch inside: John Bonus is content in his buffet-spread of fungi and insects. He is as surprised as I am to find himself here.

There are those who would say it might bring bad luck not to close the catacombs behind us. I thank Colin. The sun falls onto me like familiar clothing. Across the open land in front of us Henry Tate's and John Doulton's mausolea absorb the late afternoon heat. These retired merchants have time to revel in their legacy. Light stencils the ground between them and us. The fox has gone. Goldfinches dart between trees.

DOCUMENT D : CONCEPTION

Poets should never be buried in the earth with a mortsafe
across : their texts are metallic frames for body snatchers
to loot. There are ways around this today; surveillance
is low : the overground is ill-aware of those beneath.
Bad poets nip the lungs of the originals. Defibrillation;
mouth-to-mouth : poets are vampyres. This time there's no
phone call but, instead, a letter.

> *Dear Daniel Rush Esq*
> *I write to you with the esteemed respect*
> *worthy of one who has inspired me to do so,*
> *from a place as far away as I am. It is*
> *in admiration of your art and through your*
> *admittance that, like myself, you are not*
> *an original so much as a passionate re-maker*
> *of the works that have inspired you to live.*
> *It's of this that I speak: I am sending you*
> *one of my poems and would be perpetually*
> *grateful if you would be so kind as to lay*
> *it to rest above the ground where I am*
> *buried in the South Metropolitan Cemetery,*
> *Norwood, adjacent to where you currently*
> *reside. I was for so long distanced from*
> *the need to create in my life, matters*
> *both personal and ecumenical very often*
> *waylaid me from all things poetical, that*
> *to closely feel the words that I myself*
> *wrote when my blood flowed thick and strong*
> *would be of great relief to me.*
> *Yours with the greatest sincerity*
> *John Yarrow*

I read the poem. The poem reads me:

> *Language is mute; my bosom throbs with*
>   *fear*
> *While contemplating the conception grand*
> *That hath for centuries amaz'd our land*
>   *and*
> *Nor ours alone. The list'ning earth*
>   *accords*
> *Spontaneous admiration : some, stand*
> *Stricken with wonder some murmur solemn*
>   *words,*
> *Or, breathe, in awe. His name, whose mind*
>   *such wealth affords!*

The words are familiar, the false ictus of each stress
rises with my blood : I wrote this poem. Twenty years ago,
when I started out, I had a bad teacher who encouraged
my admiration for the Augustans, particularly Dryden.
This was in the days before I had my breakthrough and re-
appropriated my art into the true work of the conceptualist,
the cut-and-paste-ist, the artist-of-ideas. Before the
new identity & the wet warfare with the middle-stream
of the river. I was writing 'verse' as tight and formal
as Rubiks, cubing the pork joint of life into regulated
lardons. Could it really be that I was two hundred and
fifteen years behind my time? How could I be that far
behind & now be so far ahead? Can a man jump through time-
barriers during the mid-point of their life?
    My body, my work. My body of work.
    I dig out the poem from my archives & scan the
lines. I walk straight onto the 76 bus on Norwood High
Street & it clatters through the rush hour towards King's

Cross, trundling like a cattle-shed. I read the poem.
The poems reads me. I knew what the poem said before I
wrote it : only a poet would know what that means. I was
born with the poem in my gums, waiting for its moment,
for the baby-teeth of my goo-goo language to make space
for the blocks of text. I walk though the courtyard of
the library, past the pagodas of learning & Newton's
gravitational slump. I call up the books, showing my card
: JOHN YARROW. The librarian doesn't flinch. Eight books
in my name, under my name, issued to my name.

    I flick them : the goat-leather covers stick to
the fingers. One of them shows Yarrow's date of birth
: February 27th. My date of birth, Alex Lumis. I find
the poem — his poem, my poem — it's part of his epic
Shakespeare: A Tercentenary Poem. I take out my version
and scan the lines : 'Language is mute', 'conception
grand', 'whose mind such wealth affords'. The same in
all parts. Each stress, each beat. The metrics, the
syntax. My choice, his choice. The only difference is his
original use of 'admiration' instead of 'satisfaction' in
the fifth line.

    How right I was to regroup my practice. To make my
writing a writing of ideas, a new approach to dead words.
I cut out each word from the opening of his poem — the
man on desk 453 opposite looks up from his laptop with
that look I've seen before : the learner frightened by
the creator — as I place each word out on the table in
front of me in a shattered tower of windows. I make the
poem again. My poem, his poem:

Language	*throbs*	*earth*	*in*	*awe*
For	*centuries*	*the*	*land*	*with*
Fear	*is*	*mute*	*contemplating*	
Spontaneous	*wonder*	*the*	*conception*	

Accords   solemn   wealth   affords   stricken
Breathe   whose   name   is   ours

This is the poet I've become : the one unoriginal
luminary.
        Two black suits pull me from my seat, backwards
into a room of cameras & documents. There are dozens of
screens & on the wall there's a postcard with an image
of the Parthenon with *Athens* written in Comic Sans. They
ask me questions. Their questions, my silence.
        Their questions, my silence.
        Their silence, my silence.

Part 4
Spillways: Journeys Out from the Cemetery

But worse than all hitherto mentioned, is the Effra river, which, taking its rise at the foot of the Norwood Hills, runs through Dulwich, and at the Police station, which is situated directly over it, reaches the Brixton Road, along the north side of which it takes its course, passes on the south side of Kennington churchyard, thence under the Clapham Road, and makes its way to the Thames, discharging itself at Vauxhall. Throughout its passage, two-thirds of which not being closed in are exposed to the sun's rays, it forms the public sewer, the common receptacle of four miles of every conceivable filth, including the unctuous oozings of the churchyard. Its slimy waters may be seen moving along, or in dry weather gathered in stagnant puddles, black as ink and with abominable putridity, whose noxiousness may be tested at the present moment by any person willing to subject his olfactory organs to such an odious ordeal.

From a letter in *The Times* written by a Lambeth district-surgeon, quoted in William Tait's *Edinburgh Magazine*, 1848

At the Pines: Visiting Swinburne and Watts-Dunton

He worked over Tristram
in fits and starts
Love and refrain of wind and
sea its intellectual
purpose in spirit Tristram
is ecstatic song if
printed and confined
Love's sail is black

Padding about in socks
"O God if there is a
God which there isn't
where are my damn boots"

        from *Pierce-Arrow*, Susan Howe

THE MAP OF THE MAGNIFICENT SEVEN contains tributaries — or perhaps veins — that link the dead poets of the cemeteries with the places they are known for writing, loving and drinking in life. Some of these places have blue plaques: these are signs of still-read poets. The discovery of Theodore Watts-Dunton and his rescuing of Algernon Swinburne takes me on a diversion from the cemetery and towards the house they lived in together in Putney. Having seen so many horizontal caskets I want to look up at the house a poet wrote in: to look for the shadows of the living behind the funereal glaze of words and inscriptions.

Watts-Dunton's wife Clara later wrote a book about this domestic set-up called *The Home Life of Swinburne*. It recounts the first meeting between the two men in which Watts-Dunton had visited Swinburne at his lodgings on Great James Street near Bedford Row in Bloomsbury:

> He found Swinburne stark naked with his aureole of red hair flying round his head, performing a Dionysian dance, all by himself in front of a large looking glass. Swinburne perceived the intruder, he rushed at him, and before Watts-Dunton could offer any explanation or deliver his introduction, [Swinburne] was flying in panic helter-skelter down the stairs.

If the stereotype of 'the critic' and 'the poet' could be captured in a real-life anecdote, this is it.

Watts-Dunton was a reassuring presence to Swinburne; the critic was a solicitor who had already taken care of some legal matters for Dante Rossetti. He had also written a very rare positive review of Swinburne's poems. Swinburne felt he could trust him on every front. Still, they were an unlikely alliance: the older patriotic solicitor and critic, and the notorious poet of the new generation whose collection of 1866 — *Poems and Ballads* — had caused such uproar with its poems about lesbian eroticism, sadomasochistic sex and necrophilia. There's no doubt that the idea of saving the younger poet was attractive to Watts-Dunton. If there were any other doubts in his mind as to the wisdom of the venture of inviting the poet to live with him, Lady Swinburne offered to pay him £200 a year towards the upkeep of the poet. It was a fait accompli.

Swinburne caricatured in *Vanity Fair*, 1874.

Swinburne, who was a recognised figure around Bloomsbury, regularly seen falling drunkenly out of taxis in a slump of red hair and green silks — a cicada flamed with brandy — was instantly missed. London silenced. Then rumours began to circulate that Watts-Dunton had abducted him. In reality, Watts-Dunton was working on reducing the poet's intoxication by alcohol using a powerful technique that was just as addictive to the poet's synapses: artistic praise. Donald Thomas details the cunning stages in which Watts-Dunton downgraded Swinburne from his staple daily brandy-by-the-bottle to just a bottle of Bass at lunch. He began by coaxing Swinburne towards port — the drink of Tennyson — and then to claret, a drink that only a good palette could appreciate. Then came the beer, its selling point being its Britishness. This was a good technique in rousing Swinburne's civic pride. The *enfant terrible* of mid-Victorian poetry started to grow fat and became increasingly deaf. Constant praise can have that affect.

During the years that Swinburne lived with Watts-Dunton

at The Pines the older poet referred to the poet-in-his-care as simply The Bard. Edmund Gosse, in the first biography of Swinburne, suggests that the pastoral care offered by the old solicitor was not always of the sagest kind; at least, it may have been good for keeping him out of trouble, but was not in any way beneficial to Swinburne's gift and purpose of writing poetry:

> The temperament of Watts, which was more practical and vigorous than his own, exercised an unceasing well-meant pressure upon Swinburne, so that the poet grew to be little more than the beautiful ghost of what he had been in earlier years.

Watts-Dunton had the confidence of Tennyson, was friends with Dante Rossetti and knew Whistler. Although guests were fewer and further between after Watts-Dunton had positioned himself as carer to Swinburne, Whistler had once dropped him a line asking 'Dear Theodore, Watts-Dunton?' This would have been meant as a sneering jibe to Watts-Dunton who had only taken the 'Dunton' of his mother's maiden-name in 1897 when he was in his 70s. Whistler had become the shock victim of an attack from Swinburne 10 years before when Swinburne published an article in the *Fortnightly Review* attacking the artist's work. They had been friends in the 1860s when Swinburne had written a poem in defence of Whistler's picture 'The Little White Girl'. Watts-Dunton confessed to Edmund Gosse that 'I persuaded Swinburne to write the really brilliant article'. The caring critic was quite capable of stirring rancour — especially towards radical American artists.

The best of Swinburne's poetry is worth looking at closely for its technical innovation and urgency. He is a fascinating poet of in-between places. Like many of his peers his work seems concerned with ancient myth and Medievalism; yet, like Hopkins, he is a poet capable of climbing inside natural landscape to return with the experience held in his hands in rich chunks of language. He wrote his poems at speed (the 160 lines of his poem 'Faustine' were apparently written on a train between Waterloo and Hampton Court) and often outdoors, drawing the specifics of wind and light into the swoop of his lilting lines. Edgeland cliffs, seaside coves and hidden gardens all feature. He was an explorer of the little trodden paths, hidden byways. He also took this fascination with in-betweeness to the furthest bounds of acceptable taste: into erotic death and the necrophilic. In 'Laus Veneris' the main character holds the body of his dead lover in his arms, lingering between the loss of her bodily satisfaction and the still-present desire to fulfil it. The poem — along with others from the same collection, focusing on Sapphic desire — contains imagery of sado-masochistic pleasure and voyeurism:

> Their blood runs round the roots of time like rain:
> She casts them forth and gathers them again;
> With nerve and bone she weaves and multiplies
> Exceeding pleasure out of extreme pain.

Swinburne is significant for pushing forward what it was acceptable to say in Victorian poetry. He is the bridge between Sade and the Surrealists. Later in life he revelled in his outsider status, writing: 'I have no apology to offer for any such aberration from the safe path of tepid praise or conventional applause'. His work is often very careless, as passages of unique, fizzing genius stumble into awkward and unresolved moments. The real and imagined exist side by side in Swinburne's work. He laughed at his critics for not realising that his work took its flight from the imagination: how could it be any other way, especially for a poet who had more in common, he argued, with a musician than a sculptor? In his earlier years he looked back to the Elizabethans and Jacobeans, to Marlowe, Webster and Shakespeare: his literary heritage was blood, sex and death.

There is an interesting cipher for gauging Swinburne's link to Modernism: James Joyce's *Ulysses*. This highly poetic novel was published in 1922 but set in 1904. Swinburne's poetry continuously recurs in the mind of Stephen Dedalus, the semi-fictional depiction of Joyce's younger self. In fact, it is 'stately, plump Buck Mulligan' — the medical student co-habiting the Martello Tower with Stephen — who first makes reference to the poet, on the third page of the book: 'God, he said quietly. Isn't the sea what Algy calls it : a great sweet mother? The snotgreen sea. The scrotumtightening sea'. An hour later, as Stephen walks Sandymount Cove — thinking about Plato's forms — the quote from Swinburne comes back to him: 'Like me, like Algy, coming down to our mighty mother'. Stephen continues to walk and as he does so he thinks in the most incredibly dense and compressed rhythms: from the reader's perspective, his thoughts are Modernist poetry. It is significant that when Stephen actually decides to write a poem on the beach, struggling to find a scrap of paper to write it on, his output is very disappointing in its overly symbolic and quaint poeticalness: 'Touch me. Soft eyes. Soft soft soft hand. I am lonely here. O, touch me soon, now'. Joyce makes a point here that the relevance of Swinburne in 1904 was much reduced by 1922. The literary development of the young poet as represented through Stephen existed in a hinge between Symbolism and Imagism (Joyce's poem 'I Hear and Army' would appear in the first Imagist anthology in 1914) reinforcing the idea that literature wasn't ready to break out of the tradition of Swinburne at this point. At least not until Stephen Dedalus had matured into Joyce. Swinburne, Joyce hints, was a poet of an old century.[35]

While Stephen Dedalus was walking Sandycove Beach on 16 June 1904, Swinburne was very likely to be drinking tea in the garden of The Pines with Watts-Dunton. His residency there can be seen as a physical embodiment of his poetic liminality: the poet lodged in Putney as if in a kind of incubus.

Watts-Dunton, left, and Swinburne in the garden at The Pines. (Radio Times Hulton Picture Library.)

Swinburne's affection for Watts-Dunton was huge and can be seen in the gushing dedication and introduction he wrote to a later edition of his first *Poems and Ballads*: 'To my best and dearest friend I dedicate the first collected edition of my poems, and to him I address what I have to say on this occasion'. Watts-Dunton was always the significant other that Swinburne wanted to impress. There is also a poem in his collection *A Century of Roundels* called 'In Guernsey to Theodore Watts'. The roundel was a poetic form that Swinburne developed later in his career and was based upon the French rondeau form, which was a common verse form set to music between 13th and 15th centuries. The form proved useful to Swinburne as it allowed him to play games with liminal states: the half-line of each stanza is familiar and assuredly unfinished. In his poem to Watts-Dunton, Swinburne — islanded in Guernsey — makes for the seaside spaces he's most familiar with:

> The heavenly bay, ringed with cliffs and moors,
> Storm-stained ravines, and crags that lawns inlay,
> Soothes as with love the rocks whose guard secures
>   The heavenly bay.
>
> O friend, shall time take ever this away,
> This blessing given of beauty that endures,
> This glory shown us, not to pass but stay?
>
> Though sight be changed for memory, love ensures
> What memory changed by love to sight, would say -
> The word that seals for ever mine and yours
>   The heavenly bay.

While this is clearly not Swinburne's greatest poem it does show how form was a useful container within which to fix his spectral and shifting fascinations, allowing him to work with urgency towards a clear, finished piece. As he explained when looking back on his poetic output: 'law, not lawlessness, is the natural condition of poetic life; but the law must itself be poetic and not pedantic, natural and not conventional'. After the ongoing epics contained in *Poems and Ballads*, it is a relief to find Swinburne working in the short contained form, even if they are only exercises in singsong. What is significant at this point in my journey is to find the poet's love for Watts-Dunton.

Swinburne's work has not endured in the same way as that of Hopkins, Browning, Tennyson and Rossetti. Watts-Dunton saved Swinburne's life but he also killed off the charge of his poetics, creating an environment of sterile advice and patriotic complacency. Without his daily brandy Swinburne's work lost its burn as well. The final 20 years of his life were a long bookend to the initial wellspring of spontaneous creativity.

The story of Swinburne and Watts-Dunton has proved useful to Susan Howe, a major experimental American poet who has researched a number of 19th century fin-de-siècle relationships in her book *Pierce-Arrow*. Howe is interested in rooting out the unsaid and the links between previously unexplored lives. She pursues the late lives of Watts-Dunton and Swinburne as if they are floating in a self-contained literary island, between the borders of the old century and the new. Her title for this section captures their hermetic literary bubble perfectly: 'The Leisure of the Theory Class'. Howe adopts an oblique technique of associations that lends itself to the strangely conjugal lives of these writers, cross-pollinating across forms through a mix of literary criticism, poetry and archival documentation that confirms many of my own thoughts on the two men — in particular Watts-Dunton's conflation of imperialism with poetry ('Silver age shaken authority / ... the golden age of poetry'). Howe also unearths some aspects that surprise me. *Pierce-Arrow* shows manuscript pages from Swinburne's poems which are attacked with crossed-out scrawls in crucifix-patterns, strikethroughs and amendments. New lines curve alongside the old — sometimes at the bottom of the page in upside-down writing — as if the page contains poetic dimensions that might only be seen through a looking glass. Howe cursorily states in one of her poems that Swinburne wrote to Arthur

Symons — a powerful link in the chain of dead poets I'm circled with — to tell him that he'd decided (after 1900) to write no more 'on imperial or patriotic subjects'. Towards the end of the sequence Howe captures the finality of closure of this late Victorian literary world when Watts-Dunton died in 1914, fittingly in the year of the outbreak of the First World War and the first Imagist manifesto:

> One evening in the spring
> of 1914 Theodore Watts-Dunton
> (his mother's maiden name
> by deed poll and hyphen)
> quietly died in his sleep
> he was resting on a sofa
> near the last best photograph

View of Swinburne's bedroom where he lived for 30 years and in which he died.

of Swinburne (Photo: Poole,
Putney) Clara Watts-Dunton
didn't remarry Swinburne's
library became her bedroom

Above the tower at the top of the house, where Watts-Dunton could hear the poet stamping in fits of inspiration before sitting to condense the moment in lyrical flow, there's a weathercock wedged stuck, facing towards the east. There's a skeletal aerial above there too, suggestive of the real world of exploration that Swinburne put behind him in the last 30 years of his life, residing in the bedroom that he barely left.

Putney is the district of dentists. Next door to The Pines is Putney Hill Dental Practice — *Nervous patients welcome.* Across the road, facing The Pines, is Gentle Dental — *the dentist with a difference!*

The gates of Theodore Watts-Dunton's residence in Putney.

They offer walk-in hygiene appointments. The neighbourhood is instilled with Watts-Dunton's spirit of cleanliness and care: at the other end of the hill is a residential home, also named The Pines, as if in homage to the philanthropic critic. I imagine nurses spoon-feeding rows of red-haired poets wrapped in green blankets.

When it was built The Pines would have stood as both a landmark and a symbol of the new outer-London building developments built around the crossroads of Putney Hill and what's now the South Circular Road. Its neighbouring terraces have been refashioned into estate agents, a dry cleaners, a *What a Chicken* fast-food outlet. A glut of teenage schoolboys sit around a table in school-hours, dipping their fingers into boxes of spiced wing and bone. They're too old for Swinburne's later-life love of children; teenagers like these would have brought to mind his own dark early years, though Swinburne never regretted the cultural brand of transgression that made his name.[36] It's tempting to think of The Pines as a kind of mind in itself, with Swinburne wildly oscillating between the ego and id as the critic plays the superego.

Next along are two estate agents. The agents themselves are ferocious single men in suits, no older than 25; they sit behind raised desks with images of cracked houses shining from laminated photographs. A residence similar to The Pines goes for just under a million. Across the road is a branch of Foxtons, the huge windows offering a vista of purple and green seats designed for a future form of travel-without-movement. A young agent — his forehead so smooth that the client's face is reflected in it — offers her a bottled Perrier water as she clammily attempts to add her signature to paper. Above the windows, on the brickwork, is a public artwork unrelated to sales, which works as the greatest subliminal message possible;

the bronze words beneath a bronze clock and swan declare: TIME LIKE AN EVER ROLLING STREAM.

I leave the waning genius and ageing critic behind, two men unready for the advent of Modernism. It is too sad to watch Swinburne's genius ebbing into afternoon chitchat and tea like this. I picture him falling from a horse-drawn cab, inflamed with brandy and the intoxicating flow of poetry that only had to end because the page has limits. I leave him on the street in Bloomsbury, in the years before The Pines, looking with awe and wonder at the passing crowds, looking at him with awe and wonder.

Following the Effra from the Graves to the New World

From the world beyond earth, from the night underground,
That scatters from wings unbeholden the weight of its darkness
Swinburne, from *Erechtheus*

IT MIGHT NOT BE, IN THE END, MORE THAN A METAPHOR: the underground river as a way of linking these dead poets to the main flow of the English canon. The poet's death as a kind of Styx of non-success, a Lethe of public forgetfulness. Poets have drawn upon the underground rivers of Greek mythology for centuries. The dead poets of West Norwood have their own underground source: the River Effra, which once flowed through what became the cemetery's grounds. The river was diverted before the cemetery was built, being rechanneled and adapted as part of Bazalgette's new sewerage system. It was pumped through a drainage gate in the crypts under St Luke's Church, where it then followed its course to Herne Hill and Brixton. There is a widely circulated story of a coffin submerging into the flow of the river and travelling down the Effra to emerge in the Thames. When the coffin was traced back to West Norwood the surface ground where the grave had come from was undisturbed.

Metaphor Two: these silenced dead poets quietly sliding in a sewer towards the majesty of the Thames, captured by the often quoted poems of the triumphant Spencer and Wordsworth. *Sweete Themmes! runne softly, till I end my Song.* The songs of the Norwood dead are in the underground flow. There is sewerage and little light, though always a chance that a casket might slip into the main stream and appear in public view at Westminster or Waterloo Bridge.

The contemporary poet U.A. Fanthorpe opens her poem on London's underground rivers with the following quote from a paper read at the Auctioneer's Institute 1907: 'A river can sometimes be diverted but is a very hard thing to lose altogether'. I am interested too in a claim by G.W. Lambert that three quarters of the city's paranormal activity takes place by buried water. Rising vapours are easily mistaken for spectres. The great poetic afterlife I'm looking for, the still living body of potent work, might need some spur from the ghosts of the dead 12. It's winter now and it's worth a go — by the Spring I'll have moved on to Nunhead Cemetery, the next bead in the chain of the Magnificent Seven.

Colin meets me early outside the gates of the cemetery: the air today has the metallic bite of new beginnings. Despite the hangover I've inherited from late-night drinking with living poets we are both, this morning, men of purpose. Colin leads me to a modern drain

Colin pointing in the direction of the flow of the Effra towards Herne Hill.

cover, identifying it as the spot where the Effra would have flowed before its redirecting in the 1830s.

Colin points towards the adjacent St Luke's beneath which the river was made to flow. In the summer, when I'd visited to gift the poets their stones, Colin's small red cap had defined the fizz and buoyancy of the moment: today it's his black leather gloves. This lends his words the extra articulation of his hands; the stories of the dead are there to be sung, and conducted for the full aria of their epic lives.

Originally the river would have flowed, he says, under the mausoleum of Sophie Beard, an impressive hut-like monument behind him. Later, I look her up and find her monument is listed by English Heritage: 'Mausoleum in form of a Gothic chapel. Sophie Beard died in 1850, chapel somewhat later; architect unknown. Portland stone'. The entry continues with the kind of ornate language that the architecture invites: 'Plank door with elaborate wrought iron scroll pattern hinges and decorative ironwork ... Above the entrance

Sunlight streaming on the face of Faith on the mausoleum of Sophie Beard .

a trefoil light with shaped hood mould. Trefoil lights on the rear elevation have original stained glass'. The monument was paid for by her two sons and etched on the columns on either side of the door: 'Erected as a last testament of love / To the memory of a perfect wife and mother'. The light streams in plated silk; transparent and illuminating the statuette of Faith.

Sophie Beard wasn't a poet. The poets aren't speaking today as I'd hoped. The reticent 12: language beyond them. I follow Colin towards the west side of the cemetery, weaving through the grass around the graves that have been saturated with the recent torrents of rain. We arrive at an above-ground Styx in which a crucifix reflects an upside-down replica of itself. It is like the gravestones themselves have rolled up their trousers and are trying to wade through the fetid water. The ground has opened on a life-or-death game of chess in which all the knights make their moves at once.

Colin is warming up now, stepping into his stride; when he's in this kind of mood it's a delight to try to stay within touching

Heavy rainfall on the gravestones above the old course of the Effra.

distance of his quickening shadow as he allows all of the synchronous strands of death's stories to tighten into one commanding rope of exploration: who ever really dies when the stories are still here to be told? He aims fire with his right glove towards a tree or a grave, but it's the course of the Effra he's charting, not forgetting the purpose of my visit.

Colin's leather gloves have me fixed in their display of Victoriana authority: there is, after all — and as I'd hoped — magic at work in the language today.

Colin's next suggestion brings back the memory of his invite to the catacombs in the summer: "We could," he suggests, "drive down to Dulwich and find where the Effra shows itself?". He's done this before and knows I won't say No. As we leave the cemetery he points out a small monument made by Doulton. It's smaller than a coffee table but its impact is huge; an angelic figure is set in motion above the azure blue and marble clouds. There is something else here too: what seems like a poem. After months of searching the cemetery I've not seen a complete stanza of poetry set into the stone before. The angel's arm defines its own space away from the main inscription:

> On that happy Easter morning
> All the graves their dead restore
> Father, sister, child and mother
> Meet once more

The prevailing Tennysonian octosyllabic. The 'happy' is too prescriptive of emotion but I like the enjambment that rolls 'their dead restore' to the reuniting of the family in 'Father, sister, child and mother'.

The grave of Amelia McKeown designed by Doulton.

Graveside, I take out my Blackberry and open the internet: the 3G reaches up into the winged air of the still living and connects the questions of the dead with Google's infinity of answers.

Disappointingly the poem isn't a poem but a part of a hymn called 'On the Resurrection Morning', written by Sabine Baring-Gould (1834-1924). The poem continues in the vein of the snippet on the grave. Even in hymns the customary Tennysonian form prevailed and to read it as a poem shows the piece — like so much of what I've found — to be well-made and capable of fulfilling its function as a capsule for grief and mourning. The piece was set to music and published in the *Church Times* in 1864. It was also played on the Titanic: resurrection and submersion coalesce in my mind.

I look up Sabine Baring-Gould. He was an Anglican Priest and also a novelist and scholar with a bibliography that contains over 1,200 publications. As well as hymns, he wrote folk songs and collaborated with Cecil Sharp on the collection *English Folk Songs for Schools* (published in 1907): his reach, it's fair to say, went well beyond any of the 12 poets here, hence why he appears in cameo on somebody else's tomb. As well as writing novels there is another poetry link with Baring-Gould: he wrote the biography of the poet-priest Robert Stephen Hawker, who was made famous through his poem 'The Song of the Western Men' with its refrain: "And shall Trelawny die? / Here's twenty thousand Cornish men / will know the reason why!". Dickens had published this anonymously in *Household Words* but later gave away the poet's name. Hawkins is the kind of eccentric that poetry through the ages has attracted: he only wore bright clothes (at his funeral in 1875 everyone wore purple instead of black), often dressed as a mermaid, kept a pig as a pet and excommunicated his cats from catching mice on Sundays. His hut — known as Hawker's Hut — can still be visited on the cliffs overlooking the Atlantic. Hawker would go there to write his poems and letters but was unorthodox in always ensuring that bodies of men that washed up from shipwrecks were given a proper service and burial (it would have been impossible to know if they were dissenters). He had married his first wife when he was 19 and she was 41 and when she later died he reversed the mismatch, re-marrying a girl of 20.

This is the kind of connection that happens when walking with Colin: coincidence becomes a kind of spade with which it's possible to dig back with, into past earth. Yet despite the delight of finding Hawker as a character, Baring-Gould's cameo here does not bear the fruit of poetry. As well as hymns and folk songs he also wrote novels and ghost stories and an often cited book on lycanthropy. When his wife died in 1916 — his teenage love — he had inscribed on her gravestone: 'half my soul'.

The Effra waits for us. We walk out from the cemetery, along Norwood Road and follow the current flow of the river, past the steam engine parade of green stench-pipes. When Colin is out driving, he tells me, he shouts "stench-pipe" whenever he spots one of the columns appearing on the horizon. These 50-feet-high pipes were built to allow methane and other noxious gases to escape from sewers and underground rivers — which became the same thing after Bazalgette's project to address the stink of London. We walk past a round, hut-like building on the corner of Pilgrim Street called The Boat House. There is a legend that Queen Elizabeth sailed up the Effra to visit Walter Raleigh at Brixton. We turn before Elder Road, where there's a famous landmark up the side of a building which reads: FLOOD LEVEL 17th July 1890. The Effra's legacy is written along the extant architecture here. As in the quote used in the Fanthorpe poem above, it has been diverted but not lost.

Colin lives a few roads back from the cemetery. We head to his car to drive towards Belair Park and the opening of the Effra. We walk through an estate of barbed wire and prefabricated huts, one of which is a revivalist church. I've never felt it necessary to go the edge of anywhere to find what's often called an *edgeland*: these interzone spaces occur so unexpectedly in London that the mind of anyone walking through the city has to be resilient to the speed of atmospheric change.

Colin gets into his car and takes off his gloves, placing them on the dashboard. His cap follows: I notice it says WILDERNESS across the front. Our orchestration of the dead is done for now. The roads steeply decline towards Belair Park.

Belair Park is like any other London Park. There are children's swings and slides and a football pitch. People are walking their dogs. Like many other London Parks there is a small lake too; this one has the signs: PLEASE DO NOT FEED THE WATERFOWL and NO PRACTISING GOLF. There are Canadian geese and coots in buoyant expectancy of bread.

Colin's gloves resting on the dashboard between the route of the hidden Effra and its opening.

There's a small red lifebelt attached to a rope, should it be needed.

"This is it," Colin says: "the Effra."

There's a man standing next to us with a clipboard and a laminated letter which he's trying to pin to the railings around the water. Colin has gone quiet; I can sense his curiosity drawing towards the letter. The moment's never to be missed, connections don't happen to the sleepwalking — he walks across and asks what he's doing. The council official explains. There are known five-year and additional 75-year 'flood events' that take place around the Effra. He explains that as rainfall runs into the Effra the river can overflow, leaving the surrounding areas vulnerable to flooding. He cites the recent torrents as evidence of the necessity of the work to be carried out. The work, he says, will consist of localised earth modelling including the creation of low earth bunds, spillways and a detention basin. There is a one-sentence caveat to the Good Works proposed: the work might change the conservation aspect of the area.[37] The official trusts us to a map of the works which I photograph with a hack journalist's ruthlessness. Our search for an old lost river ends with the realisation that the Effra is real, that what might seem obscure and hidden is as capable of impact as anything newly built above ground. I think of Menella Bute Smedley and the brilliance of her best work.

Council official showing a map of the work required around the current Effra.

We head back to Colin's Skoda. There is certain kind of adrenalin that comes from these collisions between the old and new worlds. Colin drives me to Herne Hill station, the end point of today's journey. As we move through the smooth, pre-rush hour traffic, he explains some basics of hydrology to me — an illuminating gift given my background in poetics. "Stench-pipe" he shouts out — pointing to the green stanchion across the road — before picking up the point he was making about attenuation and rainfall.

Everything is on the hoof with Colin, even being a passenger. He stops at the lights of a busy junction between the road to Brixton and Herne Hill station. It's not a good place to park, he says, and I ask where I should get out: "Here?" he asks. He's given so much of his time to me I don't question it. I grab my bag and open the door and emerge in what seems like the middle of a dual carriageway. The strange speed of London's byways is exactly as Ballard depicted them. I weave between the streams of traffic and make for the nearest concrete island.

DOCUMENT E : CONFESSION

My archive, my iPad. My epic, my lyric. My manuscript, my backup.

    I fall asleep at night with my back to the firewall. I've found another old poem in my archives — the archives that the British Library will one day pay me for. It's called *The Leaves of Everything : a Fragment*. The lines rove in the pentameter I aspired to at the time:

> *And then with wonder near to full clear sense*
> *I dug into myself : saw clear my face*

On the way from the building I take the Victorian coal shovel from the communal fireplace in the hall. Norwood High Street is swirling with revellers & hungering taxis. I have an Effra in my heart : sometimes it floods.

    All my works have been leading to this : the summer when I watched David Blaine grow sallow & fat in his box over the Thames for 44 days. I wrote a poem to the sun each day.

    When Norwood closes its gates in the evening the easy route is over the railings. The railings made to keep the body snatchers out. I've walked here before, past the Maddick Musuem & around the back of the reception. John Yarrow's tomb has the force of an early Modernist object : its title-text positioned less than halfway down, its stone canvas just off-white.

    A crow — or a jay — cracks the hollowed-out twigs of its wings. A fox freezes in its cement-set of concentration. The wind oozes thin through the thorn from Norward.

    The torch lightens my name : Yarrow.

I set the camera to stream live to my website & open a
separate browser on my tablet so I can follow the analytics
: my audience, my art. I take out *In Memoriam* from my
jacket & between each scrape of the spade, read:

> *Old yew*

Schraahr

> *Which graspest at the stones*

Shcgararrrrrr

> *That name the under-lying dead*

Shraarrp

> *Thy fibres net the dreamless head*

Schafarpppppp

> *Thy roots are wrapped about the bones*

Shcraffhhhhd

Tracker : 23 visitors. A happening.

> *The seasons bring the flower again*

Shraffffchp

> *And bring the firstling to the flock*

Schccraarrpppp

And in the dusk of thee, the clock
beats out the lives of men

Visitors : 54. My conception, my followers.

O not for thee the glow, the bloom

Schrafff

Who changest not in any gale

Schrraarrpppp

Nor branding summer suns avail

Scraaaafffppp

Visitors: 113. My figures, my words.

To touch thy thousand years of gloom

Schraaaafffppp

And gazing on thee, sullen tree

Scrhatrffffp

Sick for thy stubborn hardihood

Scraffapphhrrrr

I seem to fail from out my blood
And grow incorporate into thee

The coal shovel hits solid. 267 visitors. I position the camera towards the grave. Their poet, my poet. I speak into the camera : "Welcome to Unpoetic Digging : a live conceptual poetry performance by John Yarrow". My hat drops into the opened earth. I wipe the soil from my upper lip. My face, his face. His face, my force.

The wood is masticated with earth, the lid is sodden : pocked with beetles & the wet gloss of earthworms. My genius has been to simply remove soil : the coffin was already open. I scratch off the remaining granules & lift the splintered bars of wood.

"The skeleton has its own syntax", I say to the camera : "& all previous syntax is available for use". The outline of the jaw has the oratorical gravitas of mine. Same tooth missing : upper molar right.

Visitors : 843.

A house alarm whirls over Norwood High Street. The jay turns sleeplessly in its bed of quills.

Across the sternum of the corpse is a page, yellowed & foxed; the phalanges of my hand reach down & pull it up towards my clavicle. I take back what's mine & shine the torchlight on the paper:

THE LEAVES OF EVERYTHING

And then with wonder near to full clear sense
I dug into myself and — at last! — saw clear my
                                    face.

Whiston Wood

THERE'S A BOOK BEHIND THIS BOOK. This book stalls. The book behind this book is a different book; a book set outside of London. Unexpectedly, at the end point of the year, there's a block against facing death. I've spent too much time with the dead this year. Something's bothering me: a death behind all the other deaths, a stone that should be more familiar than Yarrow, Capetanakis, Smedley. I can't see that stone for all of these stones.

When we die, I figure, we're always being driven. It is dark and the moving road is lulling, even to the most anxiously bereaved. There are cars passing towards us and the radio's playing a song by Bob Dylan. The internal fan heater spins its warm narcotic. You realise you've always loved being driven — the faster the better. The passenger seat is where the sharp hurtful edges of existence — work, commitments, responsibilities — blur into distant trees. The only sounds are the sounds you want right now: the engine's warm cycle, the rasp of the singing voice. Between songs the occasional birdsong breaks the silence of the dashboard.

We're passing the edge of Whiston Wood, following the course of Whiston Brook: a stream so ancient that Google can't source it beyond the Properties For Sale in the area. Skylarks take up their singular sentry-points and on the horizon — a selling point for estate agents — is a view of Halton Castle. There are so many ox-eye daises in the woods they are viewable from space. Or at least on Google Maps. A white line discernible with a tap or two of the zoom function.

When we die we're always being driven. Except here, on

this trip, I'm long past the worst of bereavement and I'm not dead — my dad is. And there is no complete calm in the car, even though my brother is driving and would sacrifice the spoken word for the sound of the music. My son, Pavel, is talking in the backseat, asking questions across the neck-rest between us. How many days, he asks, did I cry for when my dad died?

I tell him it's not a simple as that; that we all cried but that we also thought back with some happiness — at the memories, the strange things that happened — and laughed too. That sometimes, 10 years later, we still cry. Pavel's sitting next to my mum, who's flying to Lanzarote with her partner in the morning. Christmas gatherings have arrived earlier than usual.

My dad was always the driver. Long motorway journeys beginning in the dark and ending in low-light. Radio plays acted out in accents that didn't sound like anyone we knew. The seat belt catching my slumping shoulder. I felt safe then, being driven: the faster we go, the better. We pass the signs too quickly to read them. The driver — my dad — always had the map in his head so we could relax.

We walk to the gates in the dark of the year, in the week before Christmas. There's a side-door open for late visitors. My brother gives my son the torch. I link arms with my mum. There are black pools of stagnant water on the path — this path with no Victorian history — and we walk forwards, like late-comers at a play looking for our seat, searching with the torch for the right row, for evidence of my dad's headstone. The grass is light and aerated beneath us, like AstroTurf. There are other torches in the distance, low to the ground, like miners rising from the earth's crust.

Our torch flashes at a stone which shows the shape of a

teddy bear. A life that expired after months. Then a straightforward simple stone for a long-living Agnes. Sometimes my brother, a night-working taxi driver, comes here after midnight for a smoke, knowing he's unlikely to be buzzed for a job as he's so far from the centre of Liverpool. Hanging out in cemeteries must be a family thing. Despite his familiarity with this place after dark he is also having trouble spotting the headstone. We've lost our dad.

It's Pavel who hits the jackpot and shouts out the letters on the stone:

TREASURED MEMORIES OF
PAUL WILLIAM MCCABE
1948 - 2004

It's been a while since I've been here, in this different book. This is the book that isn't about poets though my dad wrote one or two poems and brought Shakespeare, Joyce and Dylan Thomas to our home.[38] This was against the grain of his upbringing and the always pressing need to make money. When he brought home the three-volume *Oxford Treasury of English Poetry* we teased him about it, asked him Why? "It's good" he said. "Some of it". My journey into the other book has been worth it for Menella Bute Smedley alone: an addition to the minority of known good poetry in the world. I have lost a great dad who was not a good poet, and have found a good, but not a great, poet.

Since that day in 2004 when we came to put him in the ground the headstones have expanded across the grass, as if someone's just been picking up what was already lying flat on the earth: dominos placed upright. In this different book — the one I've not been writing — I realise that I have been moving away from the simple hard fact of its text. The torch scans down the headstone to: DIED AGED 55 YEARS.

And, I realise now, this book I *have* been writing has a different ending to what I expected. I realise that if I'd have written this ending in the past, or if I tried again in the future, that too would be a different ending. The ending will always be changing because Pavel — aged six, stands here for the first time, on his unexpected journey into death, wearing Wellingtons with his school uniform — will have so many questions to challenge any settled understanding of my dad's death. The questions ring from him quicker than I can answer them: "Is the word 'grandfather' on the stone for me?" he asks. "But how can it be when he never met me?", " And where is he anyway?", "Can we open up the ground?", "How can we see him?", "Well let's imagine that it wasn't illegal, what would he look like?", "Is he still wearing his glasses?"

I laugh at this last question, in this different book, because I picture my dad as a kind of calcified Buddy Holly, a musician he loved when he was a teenager. Cars pass alongside the cemetery wall, the happy ones locked in their warm boxes of light and sound. The contented ones being driven.

Pavel asks why he died when he was 55 when people should live until 100? I think of my dead poets in Norwood: seven of the 12 outlived my dad and that was back in the age of cholera and unsanitary medical techniques. We're told all the time that 'we' are living much longer as a nation. There's nothing statistical about the death of your father. My son's fascination with death has been growing. When I came back from London a few weeks ago he had something urgent to tell me, news that I had obviously never heard — if I *had* heard this, I would have told him — "Guess what?" he said, "when people die they put them in *boxes*!"

I stand with my mum and brother planning the next summer, in this different book, when we'll come back in the 10th year after his death — the whole family — and picnic together in the grounds. There will be skylarks above us, the dash of a fox, and we'll raise a glass of his favourite drink: a vodka. I tell them it's possible to adopt a tree in the next field, Whiston Wood, and have his name written into it.

As we walk away Pavel tries to take a wrong path in the darkness and we lure him back from the woodlands. In the hush of the car the heat hits us. My mum says that she might not bother sleeping before her early flight tonight, maybe a few hours on the sofa. We pass a funeral directors which carries the euphemism which might be a good title for this book I'm not writing: MONUMENTAL CONSULTANTS.

We are on the fringe of Liverpool, heading home towards the centre of the city. The direction I'll take on my journey through the Magnificent Seven cemeteries will be from south London to north, up from West Norwood to Nunhead, then on to Brompton, Kensal Green, Tower Hamlets, Abney Park and Highgate. The direction will always be northwards towards Euston and the trip back home, to Liverpool. Towards the book I have to learn to write.

For now I relax.

I love being driven.

ENDNOTES

[1] Despite his criticism of Hopkins during the latter's lifetime, Bridges began to be influenced by his work; like a good anti-ageing collagen the influence crept from Bridges' bedchamber as he slept and tightened his poems in near-readiness for the world after Modernism. Bridges' poem 'London Snow' shows the influence of Hopkins in its counterpointing of an irregular internal stress pattern with regular rhymed stanzas.

[2] Swinburne once boasted that he'd enjoyed pederasty with a monkey and then eaten the monkey's corpse.

[3] Gordon claims that Dickinson suffered from epilepsy and that she struggled to keep her seizures secret. Gordon's argument has been refuted by a number of critics yet her book offers strong evidence — such as the poet's aversion to daylight and her practice of writing at night; as well as the prevalence of the illness in her family — to suggest that this struggle in her provided a high-wire tension between the seeming order and simplicity of her life and the explosiveness of her poems.

[4] These late poems of despair have become known as the 'terrible sonnets', though not because of their quality: as Hopkins' friend R.W. Dixon said, they reached 'the terrible crystal', capturing — almost in quartz — the despair that Hopkins was living through at this time.

[5] The 'voice' of the poet is an often over-used term in prosody. I would like to define this specifically as relating to the distinct stylistic techniques that the poet develops to make their work sound like no other's. When considering so much Victorian poetry, it is clear that the overuse of closed metrical forms — such as the octosyllabic lines — makes it impossible for the majority of poets to sound unique. We hear the echoing pastiche of those who came before. Tennyson was an exception. The regularity of stresses

within the line becomes a cage from which it was impossible for the poet to escape. This is why Hopkins' questioning of this 'same and tame' approach opened up a new way of allowing his work to draw closer to the surprise, inflection and variety we hear in speech. His use of Reversed Feet and Counterpoint Rhythm meant that he could, first of all, surprise the reader's sense of what would come next and, secondly, was capable of controlling the reader through slowing down and speeding up his poems as necessary. The distinction should be made between 'voice' and 'speech' here because although there is very often a direct colloquial address in Hopkins' poems, he makes space for himself to do this through a denser, more syntactically compressed language than we would ever hear in conversation. Yet when it's read aloud, the power of musical stress-patterning gives the work its charge. The space he's made is the antithesis of the textual cage of the average Victorian poet.

[6] Dickinson saw only a dozen of her 1,800 poems published before her death, and when they did come in to print they were significantly hacked by publishers to make them adhere to the conventions of the time. Her technical brilliance — the free use of dashes like motorway cats eyes when passed at speed — were written off as mistakes.

[7] Higginson was editor of *Atlantic Monthly*. He had asked young writers to send work and Dickinson had sent four poems asking 'Are you too deeply occupied to say if my Verse is alive?' Higginson responded offering some 'surgery' of the poems, and then, in another letter, offered high praise but warned against her publishing them due to their unconventional form and style. Higginson became something of a mentor to Dickinson and, after her death, worked with the much maligned Mabel Loomis Todd — mistress of Dickinson's brother — to edit the first volumes of her work. Dickinson's unique punctuation, diction and rhyme — the marks of her originality — were heavily altered to create a more formal impression on the reader.

[8] When talking of Dickinson's 'readership' I mean her later, general readership that was not personally known to her. She did in fact have, in life,

a circle of known correspondents whom she groomed as an audience. This intimate circle was massively important to her — like all poets she needed attention and praise to inspire her to make more work.

[9] It is Tennyson's earlier epic poem 'The Princess' that offers his most impressive contribution to the development of modern poetry. This poem — which imagines a women's only college set in the past (though the medieval past it describes seems more like a possible future, not dissimilar to that in H.G. Wells' *The Time Machine*). 'The Princess' is subtitled 'A Medley' and invites comparisons to later Modernist works, for example Joseph Conrad's *Heart of Darkness*. In 'The Princess' three young men, including The Prince, break into the college by dressing as women and later recount what they saw through a series of improvised poetic narratives. It becomes difficult to tell the voice of The Prince from those of the other characters. Tennyson, in the 'Conclusion', adds another layer of complexity in suggesting that the story we have just read has been 'written up' by a narrator. Bernard Bergonzi suggests that it is Tennyson's struggle with the live and complex issue of women's rights which leads him into such a tight — and interesting — direction with the form of the poem.

[10] His first book *Pauline* had been published in 1833 and his seminal *Men and Women* in 1855, though it wasn't until his long sequence *The Ring and the Book* was published in 1868 that his work began to gain a readership and receive critical praise.

[11] There were 16 poems in Lehmann's edition but the 1981 *The Isles of Greece* includes the poems 'Lines' which was found amongst Capetanakis' papers in 1958 and published in *The London Magazine* that year.

[12] Carter's idea of the unfinished aspect of his work reminds me of that other musician who's formed his own brand of urban paganism: Mark E. Smith of The Fall. He has a similar view that what gets committed to an album is just another version, no more significant that the one that is performed. There cannot be a 'better' version because there is no original. In this cascading

oeuvre of simulacrum John Peel somehow managed to capture The Fall at their best, year-by-year, enveloping the bitterwort of his lyrics in his studio's Herbarium. Unlike Smith (who had begun his creative life as a poet and whose words still do the things — in their compact unexpected loops — that we come to poetry for, creating brilliant poetic images: in one song the television is transformed to 'the tragic lantern') Carter has no wish to upset the flow of his sense-meaning with difficult or compacted imagery.

[13] These poems precede the New York School's development of the conversational, or colloquial, approach to poetry by 150 years.

[14] Austen's book has its moments that invite mockery too, especially through the anachronistic shift of re-reading lines such as 'At seventeen she began to curl her hair and long for balls'.

[15] Though there are many poets who advocate the opposite and spend their whole lives in the Duplo-world of redrafting — Elizabeth Bishop's 'The Moose' was redrafted over a period of 20 years — an outcome well worth the endeavour, according to many of her fans.

[16] Goldsmith's use of the verb 'grab' is interesting here and — perhaps I have spent too long in cemeteries to find myself making this leap — there is a connection, chronologically, between the arguments for a copyright law and that of a law to prevent body snatching. Talfourd was prescient in his case for a copyright law, which was introduced in 1844 (and became known as The Talfourd Act) to protect the cherished body of work that an author produced; the Anatomy Act was passed in 1832 and made body snatching illegal and, by providing sufficient bodies from the workhouse for anatomists to practise on, unnecessary. Both acts provided legal protection for the free dissemination and public cutting of the personal body, be it text or flesh.

[17] Sterne's sermons were published as *The Sermons of Yorick*.

[18] 'Goblin Market' has inspired critical readings from various feminist

angles, including that of the position of the female writer in a male market, and from a feminist Marxist position that argues that the poem allegorises the disenfranchisement of women in a male-controlled world of supply-and-demand. The poem's genius is that it captures the tensions of society at that time and condenses these tensions into a fascinatingly open-ended myth. Formally the poem works through a sinuous rhythm and lines of varying syllabic length; Rossetti uses dextrous stress patterns that fall on conversations and fizz with descriptions of fruits.

[19] When Swinburne was looking to publish *Tristram of Lyonesse* — dedicated to Watts-Dunton, 'my best friend' — the older of the two had suggested that he pack out the volume with 200 pages of lyrics on childhood and infancy so as to water-down the more salacious moments in the long love poem. This led to criticism of Swinburne's collection, although the main critique from Edmund Gosse was its 'lack of vital interest'.

[20] R.V. Holdsworth also argues for Symons' influence on Thomas Hardy. He makes the link between Hardy's famous opening from 'The Voice' 'Woman much missed, how you call to me, call me' as carrying a strong echo of Symons' 'Tears': 'Women, much loved, and always mine, / I call to you across the years'. Oscar Wilde called him 'Symons Ltd.', saying, 'I think one might risk some shares in Symons'.

[21] Other presses like Nabu Press and BiblioBazaar are bringing classics of literature back in to print, though no one is paid to proof-read the book or give it a description on its online listings; the covers are stock images of mountains or trees that can fit any content the book might hold.

[22] *The Lyrical Ballads* was published 66 years before Yarrow's poem and were 'experiments…written chiefly with a view to ascertain how far the language of conversation…is adapted to the purpose of poetic pleasure'

[23] We as far away from the common ground as it's possible to travel. The cost of one guinea for a common grave and three guineas for a private burial

are symptomatic of the Victorian mortality class structure. A family vault would have been £47, representing a far more spacious and comfortable investment. Peter Ackroyd makes the point in *London Under* that the catacombs reversed the spatial hierarchy of the 19th century class order in which the living poor were often confined to cellars and basements but in death the poor of the tenements could never afford the underground burials that the catacombs offered.

24 Swinburne's form uses nine lines, each having the same number of syllables, and has refrains after the third and final lines. The refrain is identical with the beginning of the first line and rhymes with the second line. The catacombs could easily suggest a poetic form: the evenly-paced-out rows of vaults, each with space for up to six coffins. If the bodies were replaced with syllables, and each vault was associated with a particular end-rhyme, it would be easy to write a poem walking around the catacombs.

25 I remember asking the man from the undertakers how long one kind of wood would last in the earth above another and then heard myself answer in my mind: *What the fuck does it matter?*

26 The reader will notice that I'm more than happy to follow a link to a poet if there is one percent chance that their remains are in the cemetery, but bloodline is not enough. These are the limits of my parameters: at least until my discovery of Anna Kingsford via her father.

27 Experiments on animals without the use of anaesthetic was normal practice back then; Anna later wrote about the howling of dogs throughout the cavernous halls of the Sorbonne.

28 According to Maitland — Anna's first biographer who was much maligned by the later biographer Alan Pert — her mind was at one point overtaken by a powerful Black Magic which she used to kill two Frenchmen. In past lives, Maitland claims, Anna believed herself to be Mary Magdalen, Joan of Arc and Anne Boleyn.

[29] Maitland writes in his autobiography that 'Never had I seen anyone so completely and intensely alive, or comprising so many diverse and incompatible personalities'. Anna had written to him to say: 'I want to know why I am so different from everybody else that I ever knew or read of, and especially how it is that I am so many and such different kinds of people, and which of them all I really am or ought to be. For the many me's in me are not even in agreement among themselves; but some of them actually hate each other, and some are as bad as others are good.'

[30] This may have been written by Theodore Watts-Dunton as his editorship began that year. The staid views of the piece is consistent with opinions that Watts-Dunton had expressed elsewhere.

[31] When Rimbaud arrived in Paris, following Verlaine's invitation, in September 1871, he explained to the older poet his intention to become a 'seer', or 'voyant' as it was in the French. The word provides a fascinating link between himself and Anna: as a noun it means both 'light', to 'witness' and 'inform' — everything that Kingsford believed her visions were being brought forward to do; but as an adjective it meant 'clairvoyant' (and Maitland believed that Kingsford could foresee future deaths, as well as creating them), providing a bridge between the now (the 'absolutely modern' as Rimbaud put it in *A Season in Hell*) and the future states of existence and death that both were interested in. In Maitland, Kingsford had found a companion and confidant (at least until her death, after which Maitland burnt papers and suggestions of exaggerated facts and spin appear) though Rimbaud found Verlaine a frustrating companion for one destined to be a 'voyant'.

[32] Rimbaud's sequence was only given that fixed title in 1886 by Verlaine who said that Rimbaud had used the title when talking about them.

[33] Royal College Street was the final address of Rimbaud and Verlaine and where they'd jousted to the point of sickness with each other. This was

on the other side of the park from Anna's college. It is fascinating to find these two seers occupying the same areas at slightly different times, as if sliding blindly across frosted panes of trapped energy, driven by their own discoveries and passions.

[34] *Spectropia* was a book of gothic optical illusions by J.H. Brown in 1864. It's full title was *Spectropia, or, surprising spectral illusions showing ghosts everywhere and of any colour*. The book was published by Brown as a reaction to the public fascination with spiritualism and his aim was to show that seemingly unexplained activity could be explained through tricks of the eye. Spectral illusions had been popular in Paris too and Rimbaud would have been aware of them.

[35] Despite this, the massive influence that Swinburne's musicality had on the younger Joyce should not be underestimated. Joyce's interest in the possibilities of the musicality of language has a strong precedent in Swinburne's work — Swinburne had described himself as 'an artist whose medium or material had more in common with a musician ... than with a sculptor'. Joyce's only book of poetry, *Poems Pennyeach*, has a Swinburnian fondness for alliteration and the looping of sounds, although this is a world away from the Modernist breakthrough of *Ulysses* and, in particular, the 'Sirens' section: 'bronze by gold heard the hoofirons'. *Finnegan's Wake* is a complete exploration of sound across numerous languages. Joyce had achieved things Swinburne would have balked at, yet the spur to create sculptural sound patterns has its roots in Joyce's fascination with 'Algy's' work.

[36] In later life Swinburne became obsessed with children. His collection *Studies in Song* includes poems for children aged six, seven and eight. In *Goodbye To All That*, Robert Graves recalled Swinburne mollycoddling him in his pram: the handing of the baton of English poetry came milky and sweet for Graves.

[37] I later followed this up and ask for details of the potential impact. I received

this response:

> Dear Mr McCabe,
>
> Thank you for your email. I have received comments from the architect on your query which I have summarised below:
>
> The proposed works in Belair Park will not require removal of any of the existing trees. The proposed works are not expected to disturb the local wildlife habitats, as they are in their majority located in the open grass areas. The site working areas will be securely fenced off and ecologists will assess any brush or scrub areas that need to be cleared in advance of any works. The proposed works will not affect the wildlife area by the lake; works to the footpath will be done by hand, while all site working areas will be securely fenced off.
>
> Please let me know if you have any further queries or concerns.
>
> Kind regards, Dipesh.
>
> Dipesh Patel
> Team Leader - Major Applications
>
> Development Management
> Chief Executive's Department
> London Borough of Southwark
> PO Box 64529
> London SE1P 5LX
>
> 5th Floor, Hub 2

[38] I hide this quote from one of my dad's poems, which I recall from memory, here, in the endnotes: 'Why stay at home and watch the Beeb / When you can go to Raby and see a red crested grebe'.

Selected Bibliography

Ackroyd, Peter, Dickens, *London*: Vintage, 2002

Ackroyd, Peter, *London Under*, London: Vintage, 2012

à Beckett, William, *The Siege of Dunbarton and Other Poems*, S.N.,
London, 1824

Aristotle, *The Poetics*, in Aristotle/Horace/Longinus, Stroud,
London: Penguins Books, 1965

Armstrong, Isobel (ed.), *The Major Victorian Poets: Reconsiderations*,
Lincoln: University of Nebraska Press, 1969

Beckson, Karl, *Arthur Symons: A Life*, Oxford: Clarendon Press, 1987

Bergonzi, Bernard, 'Feminism and Femininity in The Princess'
published in *The Major Victorian Poets: Reconsiderations* (ed.
Isobel Armstrong), Lincoln: University of Nebraska Press, 1969

Blanchard, Samuel Laman, *The Cemetery at Kensal Green: the grounds
& monuments*, London: Cunningham & Mortimer, 1843

Blanchard, Samuel Laman, *Lyric Offerings*, London: W. H.
Ainsworth, 1828

Blanchard, Samuel Laman, *The Poetical Works of Laman Blanchard,
with a memoir by Blanchard Jerrold*, London : Chatto & Windus,
1876

Bristow, Joseph, *The Cambridge Companion to Victorian Poetry*,
Cambridge: Cambridge University Press, 2000

Capetanakis, Demetrious, *The Isles of Greece and Other Poems*,
Athens: Denise Harvey & Company; 1981

Capetanakis, Demetrious, *A Greek Poet in England*; London: John
Lehmann; 1947

Carter, Sydney, *Green Print for Song*, London: Galliard, 1974

Cosslett, Tess (ed.), *Victorian Women Poets*, Harlow : Addison Wesley Longman Limited, 1996

Cox, Michael (Ed.), *The Concise Oxford Chronology of English Literature*, Oxford: Oxford University Press, 2004

Dickens, Charles; *Dombey and Son*, Kindle Version, Amazon Media

Dickens, Charles, *The Pickwick Papers*, Kindle Edition, Amazon Media

Dickens, Charles, *The Uncommercial Traveller*, London : Mandarin, 1991

Dickinson, Emily; Werner, Marta; Bervin, Jen; Howe, Susan (Preface); *The Gorgeous Nothings*, Christine Burgin/New Directions in association with Granary Books, 2013

Dickinson, Emily, *Poems Selected by Ted Hughes*, London: Faber, 2004

Fanthorpe, U.A., *Collected Poems 1978-2003*, Cornwall : Peterloo Poets, 2005

Fenn, Colin, *A Tale of Three Churchyards : a moving tale of London's bodies*, London : Friends of West Norwood Cemetery, 2014

Fenn, Colin R. and Slattery-Kavanagh, James, *West Norwood Cemetery's Greek Necropolis*, London: Friends of West Norwood Cemetery, 2011

Fenn, Colin R. and Slattery-Kavanagh, James, *West Norwood Cemetery's Monumental Architecture*, London: Friends of West Norwood Cemetery, 2012

Gordon, Lyndall, *Lives Like Loaded Guns: Emily Dickinson and Her Family's Feuds*, London : Virago Press, 2011

Gosse, Edmund, *The Life of Swinburne*, Cambridge: Cambridge University Press, 2011

Goldsmith, Kenneth, *Uncreative Writing: Managing Language in the Digital Age*, New York: Columbia University Press, 2011

Graham, Paul, *West Norwood Cemetery : The Dickens Connection* (with line drawings by Don Bianco), London : The Friends of West Norwood Cemetery, 1995

Hare, Humphrey, *Sketch for a Portrait of Rimbaud*, London : Brendin, [1944]

Christopher Hibbert, *Charles Dickens: The Making of a Literary Giant*; Palgrave Macmillan, 2009

Hopkins, Gerard Manley, *Poems and Prose*, London : Penguin, 1965

Hopkins, Gerard Manley, *The Poems of Gerard Manley Hopkins*, Oxford : Oxford University Press, 1970

Howe, Susan, *Pierce-Arrow*, New York : New Directions Publishing, 1999

Joyce, James, *Ulysses*, Oxford : Oxford University Press, 1993

Kingsford, Anna, *Clothed with the Sun: being the book of the illuminations of Anna (Bonus) Kingsford*; ed by Edward Maitland; New York: Frank F. Lovell & Company; 1889

Kingsford, Anna, *Health, Beauty, and the Toilet: Letters to Ladies from a Lady Doctor*, London and New York: Frederick Warne and Co, 1886

Kingsford, Anna, *The Perfect Way or The Finding of Christ by Anna (Bonus) Kingsford and Edward Maitland, Fifth Edition with Additions and a biographical preface by Samuel Hopgood Hart*, London: John M. Watkins, 1923

Kirby-Smith, H.T., *The Origins of Free Verse*, Ann Arbor : University of Michigan Press, 1996

Leighton, Angela & Reynolds, Margaret, *Victorian Women Poets: An Anthology*, Oxford : Blackwell Publishers, 1995

Lowry, Henry Dawson, *The Hundred Windows*, London : Elkin Matthews, 1904

Lowry, Henry Dawson, *The Happy Exile*, S.l. : The Bodley Head, 1898

Miles, A.H. (Ed.), *The Poets and the Poetry of the Century*, London : Hutchinson & Co., [1891-97]

Olson, Charles, *A Charles Olson Reader*, Carcanet Press, 2005

Opie, Iona and Opie, Peter (Eds), *The Oxford Book of Children's Verse*, Oxford : Oxford University Press, 1994

John Overs, *Evenings of a Working Man, Being the Occupation of his Scanty Leisure*, London : T.C. Newby, 1844

Pert, Alan; Red Cactus: *The Life of Anna Kingsford*; Watsons Bay, NSW: Books & Writers Pty Ltd, 2006

Pound, Ezra, *Lustra of Ezra Pound*, London : Elkin Mathews, 1916

Pound, Ezra, *Selected Poems and Translations*, London: Faber and Faber, 2010

Radcliffe, Ann, *The Mysteries of Udolpho*, Oxford : Oxford University Press, 1998

Reilly, Catherine W., *Mid Victorian Poetry 1860-1879: an annotated bibliography*, London: Mansell Publishing, 2000

Richards, Bernard, *English Poetry of the Victorian Period 1830-1890*, Harlow : Longman Group, 1988

Rimbaud, Arthur, *Complete Works, Selected Letters*, Chicago: University of Chicago Press, 1966

Robb, Graham, *Rimbaud*, London: Picador, 2001

Romero, George, *Night of the Living Dead*, 1968

Rossetti, Christina, *Selected Poems*, London : Penguin Books, 2008

Schlicke , Paul (ed.), *The Oxford Companion to Charles Dickens: Anniversary Edition*, Oxford : Oxford University Press, 2011

Smedley, Menella Bute (introduction), *Boarding Out and Pauper Schools: especially for girls*, London: Henry S. King & Co., 1875

Smedley, Menella Bute, *Poems Written for a Child*, London: Strahan and Co, 1868

Smedley, Menella Bute, *Poems*, London: Strahan and Co., 1868

Sterne, Laurence, *The Life and Opinions of Tristram Shandy, Gentleman*, London: Penguin Books, 1997

Swinburne, Algernon Charles, *Poems and Ballads & Atlanta in Calydon*, London: Penguin, 2000

Swinburne, Algernon Charles, *A Century of Roundels*, S.l. : Chatto & Windus, 1883

Symons, Arthur, *Writings*, Cheshire, Carcanet, 1974

Tennyson, Alfred Lord, *In Memoriam*, New York, London : W.W. Norton, 2004

Tennyson, Alfred Lord, *The Works of Alfred Lord Tennyson*, Ware: Wordsworth Editions, 2008

Thomas, Donald, *Swinburne: the Poet in his World*, London : Weidenfield and Nicolson, 1979

Tomalin, Claire, *Charles Dickens A Life*, London : Viking, 2011

Turpin, John and Knight, Derrick, *The Magnificent Seven: London's First Landscaped Cemeteries*, London : Amberley Publishing, 2011

Watts-Dunton, Theodore, *Aylwin*, London : Oxford University Press, 1909

Watts-Dunton, Theodore, *The Coming of Love and other poems*, London & New York : J. Lane, 1898

Watts-Dunton, Theodore, *Poetry and the Renascence of Wonder*, London: Herbert Jenkins, 1916

INDEX

.

Lightning Source UK Ltd.
Milton Keynes UK
UKHW022307240622
404929UK00003B/78/J